Seven Shoulders:
Taxonomizing Racism in Modern America

Sam Forster

Published in 2024 by Slaughterhouse Media, LLC
5900 Balcones Drive, Austin, TX 78731

www.slaughterhouse.press

First Print Edition: 2024

ISBN: 979-8-218-43305-5 (Paperback)

Book design by Slaughterhouse Media

The Author

Sam Forster is a Canadian-American writer who was born and raised in Edmonton, Canada.

After completing his bachelor's degree at the University of Alberta, he attended the University of Toronto, where he received an MA and served as a Graduate Fellow at the Centre for Ethics.

Throughout 2022, Forster worked as a reporter for the *Buenos Aires Times*, covering Latin American politics.

In January of 2023, he was awarded the Sutherland House Nonfiction Prize for *Americosis*, an impressionistic work of cultural commentary that was lauded in the pages of *The American Spectator* for its "*cinema verité* style." *The American Conservative* extended similar praise: "A blend of cultural analysis, data collection, and bright journalistic color, Forster offers a delicate treatment of coarse content."

In the spring of 2023, Forster reported on the Russo-Ukrainian War, filing stories from the metro-station-turned-bomb-shelters of Kyiv, as well as from the contested oblast of Zaporizhzhia.

In the winter of 2024, he traveled to the Middle East and wrote frontline dispatches for various outlets on the war between Hezbollah and Israel. He is one of few journalists who has reported on both sides of the Israeli-Lebanese Blue Line.

His work has appeared in a range of publications throughout Europe and North America, including *UnHerd, The National Post*, and the world edition of *The Spectator*.

In addition to his work as a writer, he is also a curator for a non-profit literary arts organization based in Montreal.

For K.W.,

I meant everything I said at convocation.

And for J.A., who tried to bribe me with a lifetime n-word pass in exchange for an A+ on the Regents Science Exam,

Keep going until they put you in the ground.

CONTENTS

Part Three — Shoulders Everywhere and Nowhere

PREFACE

Everyone says that their country is diverse.

Ethnic Han will claim that China is diverse because they live amongst Zhuang, Miao, and Manchu. Ethnic Finns will claim that Finland is diverse because they live amongst Swedes, Russians, and Sami. Ethnic Ugandans will claim that Uganda is diverse because they live amongst Kisimani, Zumwara, and Nyorai…

Of course, all of these internal ethnic factions are basically the same.

In a global context, there's nothing significant about the differences within these various ethnic clusters, and to the extent that the majority groups in these countries are cognizant of and animated by their differences, they're suffering from narcissistic delusion.

In a global context, nobody cares about the minutiae. *Kisimani? Zumwara? Nyorai?* I just made those words up. You probably didn't know, and you probably don't care.

Probably, you have a global, American conception of ethnicity, one that precludes you from wasting even a second of your time delineating the various tribal branches of a society as racially homogenous as Uganda.

Apart from the imperial extensions that are inextricably dependent on her (Canada, the United Kingdom, Australia, and New Zealand), America is the only country in the world that is pluralistic in any sort of deep, global sense. Nowhere else are the world's various ethnic groups represented on a scale that makes it difficult to identify an ethnic or racial majority, as is quickly becoming the case in the United States, if it isn't already the case.

Every major American city is a community of nations in and of itself, with Chinatowns, Little Caribbeans, Little Italies, and

Little Manilas all sandwiched amongst one another. These enclaves exist to protect the cultural power and relevance of specific groups of people, and they are all allowed to do so by the broader American society. Indeed, America is a melting pot, but it's also a mosaic. Not everyone assimilates, and as time goes on, it becomes harder and harder to identify cultural benchmarks against which aspiring Americans should measure themselves.

And so, it's worth reflecting on why Black-White race relations are the only interracial drama that can reliably capture the attention of the American public. When there is conflict between Mexicans and Armenians, virtually no one cares. When there is conflict between Russians and Koreans, virtually no one cares…

But when there is conflict between American Blacks and Whites, everyone makes it their problem. Corporate communication coalesces with the loudest voices of campus activism. Political movements twist and turn. Institutions are racked and reinvented. Cities become battlefields.

We only care about what happens between Blacks and Whites. That is the story of racial conflict in America.

Is this cultural preoccupation purely a matter of numbers?

That would be a compelling explanation were it not for the fact that the relationship between Blacks and Whites has not subsided as the primary subject of racial analysis even as both racial groups have subsided in demographic prominence. In relative terms, there are fewer Blacks and Whites in America than at any other point in the nation's history, and yet, our racial discourse has not evolved to become accordingly cosmopolitan and kaleidoscopic.

It's *slavery*, obviously. That's the answer. Slavery is the reason we focus our racial analysis more on Blacks and Whites than we do on other groups. It's the dark and obstinate Original Sin for which we have never fully atoned. It's the Original Sin that we have never fully processed.

Flattening America's racial landscape this forcefully can feel juvenile and frustrating, but it really is the most honest and practical way of conceptualizing the matter. And conceptualizing the matter is important if you want to know how America works. As a matter of sociological awareness, it's extremely challenging to overestimate the value of understanding the relationship between Blacks and Whites. Culturally, you are not much of an American if you don't get it.

Moreover, you aren't much of a global citizen if you don't get it…

While understanding the Black experience in America (relative to the White experience) is useful for Americans, it's also useful for the people of every other country that falls within America's cultural sphere.

The entire developed world fixates on the happenings of the United States. They cannot help themselves. With few exceptions, everything they eat, watch, read, sing, drink, and dance to is American. The celebrities they gawk at are American. The politicians they revere and revile are American. Their racial presuppositions, unsurprisingly, are American — and these presuppositions are as schematic and one-dimensional as the ones held by Americans themselves.

It is, deep down, all about Blacks, Whites, and the tenacious legacy of slavery.

In the Canadian boardroom, executives will feel a sort of subliminal force pushing them to hire the Nigerian applicant over the Kazakh applicant. Though this force is difficult for them to describe with any sort of clarity or historical coherence, they feel it. For some reason, it feels like they ought to correct for some sort of… nebulous….. errr…. ummm… errr…. some sort of….. ummm *historical injustice*?

Shouldn't the Nigerian applicant be compensated for what his ancestors went through... *err....* for what the Kazakh applicant's ancestors ...*ummmm*... did to him?

Do the executives consider that only a few generations ago the Nigerian's ancestors had never seen a Central Asian, and the Kazakh's ancestors had never seen an African?

Well... no....

In the Australian admissions office, administrators will feel a sort of subliminal force pushing them to admit the Zambian student over the Icelandic student. Again, the subliminal force is there... pushing... gnawing at consciences...

Do the administrators consider that Icelandics and Zambians have no historical familiarity with one another?

Well... no....

So what's going on here?

Instinctively, a crude sorting mechanism is implemented, one that groups Kazakhs and Icelanders with antebellum American WASPs while simultaneously grouping Nigerians and Ghanaians with antebellum American slaves. There's a superficial logic to the process, if you squint and stretch your imagination, but it's one that lacks any sort of grounding in historical or genealogical reality.

Around the world, people are LARPing as Americans because they see race as Americans see race. Around the world, racial politics are seen through America's dichromatic cultural lens.

That lens, I suspect, can be adjusted by provocative acts of commentary. It can be adjusted by reflection.

And so, on the 60th anniversary of the 1964 Civil Rights Act, the legislation that ostensibly ended America's long era of racial injustice, now seems like a good time to reflect.

A decade after the birth of BLM, now seems like a good time to reflect.

As the nation plods forward, only one fatal bicycle tumble or airstair accident away from its first affirmative action president, now seems like a good time to reflect.

Now seems as good a time as ever to attempt a description of what it's like to be Black in America, what it's like to be White in America, and how the phenomenological disparity between the two experiences frays our social fabric.

Two truths about the Black experience stand out to me:

1. American Blacks feel aggrieved about how they are treated in America.

2. On some level, that frustration has ontological grounding. On some level, the frustration isn't merely a psychological invention.

Unfortunately, if you ask people to make claims that are even slightly more specific than these, you will find yourself listening to some of the most appalling cultural diagnoses that you've ever heard. The most jarring thing is that they often don't need to be induced. Often, the fantasies will just be thrown at you unprompted.

Otherwise rational and perceptive people routinely say stuff that makes you want to lobotomize them and then yourself.

I often feel like I'm the only person within a thousand miles who understands what the word "institutional" means in the term "institutional racism." I look to the Dunning-Kruger effect for solace. I tell myself, on optimistic days, that all of the sensible people are biting their tongues.

But it's difficult to believe that other people like me exist in appreciable numbers. So much of the discourse is so unspeakably confused. So many people offer up the most deranged takes imaginable, takes that are quickly slurped up by the masses as though they are gospel.

And there are so many dishonest actors who are obviously smart enough to know what they're contributing to. There are so many people deliberately tying knots… so many slimeballs and opportunists who are deliberately muddying the waters…

If race is to be demystified for the masses, reflection is urgently needed…

… **now…**

Is there a particular reason why I should be the one to perform the reflection?

Is there a reason why my reflection is especially lucid or valuable?

Is it because I'm a genius? Is it because I'm a once-in-a-generation literary talent? Is it because I am the only American alive who has walked the streets both as a Black man and as a White man?

These reasons are not enough...

No, my ability to execute this incredibly important reflection stems from the fact that I am a moral layabout. I am inclined to describe rather than to admonish.

I am in a descriptive, apathetic mood…

….. maybe this mood is a phase of life……   or maybe this phase of life is just who I am …

Whatever the case, it isn't currently in my constitution to hector or moralize. I won't do it.

If you want to read a book that affirms your ethical intuitions about rightness or wrongness, go read something else. There is no shortage of options. Books of this genre litter the bestseller lists. They're everywhere. If you feel so inclined, pick one, and then spend hours reading about how slavery was *wrong*, how segregation was *wrong*, how microaggressions are *wrong*, and how a long list of other racial phenomena are *wrong*. Read about how ashamed we should feel. Read about what remedies might be implemented in order to alleviate the shame. If that's what you want, go for it.

But that's not the book I wrote. I didn't feel like there was a shortage of literature bemoaning America's racial history in highly emotional and moralizing terms. Words like "shameful," "depraved," and "evil" are used as frequently in existing books on race relations as words like "feather," "wing," and "beak" are used in birdwatching manuals. With few exceptions, the stuff that's out there doesn't serve the function of saying what previously *was* or what currently *is*, but rather, what *should have been*, or what *ought to be*. And while these works express strong, moving feelings about the acts that transpired, their intense moral language reduces the complexity of historical events to simple stories of good and evil. This approach sacrifices the nuanced details necessary for a fuller understanding of America's racial past and present.

Discussing race in overtly emotional and moral terms distorts the stark realities of the racial dynamics that have been so unshakably central to our cultural discourse. This emotive charge polarizes conversations, reducing the breadth of discourse to mere battles of moral and immoral. Such a binary framework oversimplifies the intricate social, economic, and historical factors that underlie racial issues, keeping genuine understanding and effective solutions out of reach.

Incidentally, it's worth noting that interest in race as a moral matter is a good indication of delusion....

What do I mean here?

The people who are most animated by the morality of race relations are invariably the people who have the most unhinged racial worldviews. The people who are most indignant and energized about the injustice of racial conflict are invariably the ones who make the most spurious racial claims, and to the extent that these people earnestly believe what they message to the world, they are out of touch. Neo-Nazis… Black Hebrew Israelites … these are the people who are most volatile… most affected… most wrong.

To truly grasp and address racial dynamics, a more measured, analytical approach is necessary — one that prioritizes methodical language and comprehensive analysis over emotional fervor and moral condemnation. This isn't to deny the moral dimension of racial injustice, but to assert that clarity, not intensity of emotion, leads to deeper insight.

Plenty of commentators have written books that fixate on the common humanity of man. Plenty of books have gone to painstaking lengths about how the beleaguered Black man is just as deserving of respect and opportunity as any other man that God put on this earth. Dwelling on that sort of thing doesn't strike me as interesting or useful. If you feel you need something like that, I don't know what to tell you.

I'm not your dad. I'm not your pastor or your priest. It isn't incumbent on me to hold your hand while you soul-search, and I wouldn't be any good at doing so even if it were.

I'm sure a lot of you will characterize this detachment as a personal flaw. I'm sure a lot of you will find it ugly, but I can't muster up the passion to cradle words like "should" or "ought."

I can only describe. I can only tell you what's happening.

That's all I can do.

That's all this is.

SEVEN SHOULDERS

INTRODUCTION

As far as I'm aware, journalistic blackface has been performed on four occasions.

The act was first performed by Ray Sprigle, a prominent investigative journalist working for *The Pittsburgh Post-Gazette* in the first half of the 20th-century.

Sprigle had gained a reputation as an exceptionally hands-on newsman after producing a number of immersive stories throughout the '30s and '40s. In 1937, he made national headlines when he exposed connections between Hugo Black, a Supreme Court nominee of Franklin D. Roosevelt, and the Ku Klux Klan. Prompted by Paul Block, the *Post-Gazette*'s publisher, Sprigle traveled to Alabama, Black's home state, to connect with James Esdale, who once held the position of Grand Dragon in the KKK. Initially hesitant, Esdale opened up to Sprigle after they discovered a mutual passion for chicken farming. This bond led Esdale to provide Sprigle with substantial evidence of Black's involvement with the Klan, a revelation that thrust the story onto the front pages of newspapers countrywide.[1]

In 1940, Sprigle crossed the Atlantic to report from London bomb shelters, documenting the Battle of Britain for a then-peacetime American public. The men and women of the London Fire Brigades and the Air Raid Precaution Service will have places of honor in "a Valhalla where the heroic dead of all ages gather to spend eternity together," Sprigle told Pittsburgh readers in October of 1940. "Not even the paladins of the Royal Air Force are giving their lives more dauntlessly and courageously … than these lads in their blue coveralls."[2]

In 1945, while meat was being rationed for the war effort, Sprigle undertook a mission to illegally buy up as much of the commodity as possible. This period of his career, during which he used the name "Alois Vondich," was critical in revealing the extent of blackmarket sales and ration stamp fraud. The man had a clear penchant for putting on disguises for the sake of a story…

In 1948, Sprigle darkened himself, adopted the alias "James Rayel Crawford," and set out to continue his streak of *avant-garde,* undercover journalism. Sprigle, or "Brother Crawford" as he came to be known in the South, traveled around the region for four weeks, keeping a detailed travelog that would later form the basis for his historic book.

Because Sprigle felt ill-equipped to embark on the tour alone, he sought assistance from the NAACP, which enthusiastically connected him with a sympathetic Black man to serve as both an escort and conduit into the Black community. With his Black guide to make local introductions and affirm his backstory, Sprigle produced one of the most exhaustive and revealing reports on the condition of Southern Blacks. For his primarily White readers, Sprigle provided a damning description of the buses, trains, plantations, shanty schoolhouses, doctors' offices, and homes of the Jim Crow states.

In 1949, the year following Sprigle's foray into the Black world, Simon & Schuster published the collection of entries as *In the Land of Jim Crow.*[3]

It's a historic book. It's an impressive book. It's a relatively unknown book.

The reviews have been mixed, but it's fair to say that it was celebrated more by self-described civil rights activists at the time of its release than it is by the people who describe themselves as civil rights activists in 2024. More on this to come…

The second occurrence of journalistic blackface garnered much more attention. 11 years after Sprigle crossed the color line, in the midst of the Civil Rights Movement, John Howard Griffin set out to write *Black Like Me.*[4]

Griffin is possibly the most interesting son America bore in the 20th century.

The old aphorism, "They just don't make 'em like him anymore," gets thrown around a lot to describe the Renaissance men of the Greatest and Silent Generations — the sort of men who somehow found time to win a war in continental Europe, father six kids, become entangled in a rum-running operation, and patent a new tractor accessory all before reaching the age of 28. Men of this era virtually always have biographies that are more impressive than their sons and grandsons. They seem to have all led impossible lives, and they seem to have all led them with impossible verve. I've read stories about a lot of these magnificent men, and none measure up to Griffin. Few come close.

Born into a musically and literarily endowed family on June 16th, 1920, in Dallas, Texas, John Howard Griffin was destined for a life marked by deep cultural engagement and intellectual curiosity. His mother, a classically trained pianist, and his father, a fine Irish tenor and former radio personality, instilled in him a profound appreciation for the arts. This early cultural immersion set the stage for his later explorations into the complex tapestry of human experience seen in racially diverse communities.

Griffin's academic journey began at R. L. Paschal High School in Fort Worth, but his thirst for broader horizons led him overseas at the tender age of 15. In Europe, he sunk himself in the rich academic offerings of the Lycée Descartes in Tours, France. His studies extended to the University of Poitiers, where he delved into French and literature, and later to the École de Médecine. Under the mentorship of Dr. Pierre Fromenty at the Asylum of Tours, Griffin explored the therapeutic potentials of music on the criminally insane, an early indication of his interdisciplinary approach to understanding human behavior.

During his time in France, Griffin also honed his expertise in medieval music, particularly Gregorian chant, through studies with the Benedictines at the Abbey of Solemnes. However, the outbreak of World War II prompted a dramatic shift in his pursuits. At 19, he joined the French Resistance as a medic, bravely aiding in the evacuation of Austrian Jews to safety, a testament to his burgeoning commitment to humanitarian causes.

The dangers of his resistance activities soon forced his return to the United States after landing on a Gestapo death list in 1940. Back home, Griffin joined the US military, serving 39 months in the Army Air Corps during which he leveraged his linguistic skills and cultural insights as a cultural observer in the Solomon Islands. While carrying out this mission, he nurtured many personal relationships, including with the Grand Chief Vutha of the Solomons, a fierce American ally and steadfast opponent of Imperial Japan. Here, Griffin's role was crucial in aiding senior officers to understand the region's strategic and cultural character. Deputized as a sort of martial anthropologist, Griffin's job was to build bridges between two vastly different peoples, and he did so extremely well.

Tragedy struck in 1945 when a Japanese bombing raid on the Indo-Pacific Island of Morotai left him blind. During the ensuing 12 years of darkness, Griffin's resilience and creative spirit flourished. He channeled his experiences and observations into his literary pursuits, producing works like the 1956 novel *Nuni*, which is based on his interactions with the tribal Islanders during the war. This period of enforced introspection and adaptation set the stage for his most famous work, a project that would once again see him span the divides that separate humanity along racial and cultural lines.[5]

The opening chapter of *Black Like Me* is set in Griffin's home office, in Mansfield, Texas, on the night of October 28th, 1959. It was on this evening, after reading a report about the rise in suicide rates of Southern Blacks, that the decision to conduct his fateful experiment was made. The findings of this report contrasted starkly with the views of Southern legislators he knew who insisted that race relations at the time were positive and harmonious. Suspecting this to be untrue but lacking the firsthand experience to present a compelling case to his White compatriots, Griffin pondered the best journalistic move he could think of:

How else except by becoming a Negro
could a White man hope to learn the truth?

In the second chapter, Griffin pitches the project to the editor of *Sepia*, an internationally distributed Negro magazine. The editor, a man sympathetic to the cause of American Blacks, warns Griffin that the proposal is extremely dangerous. He tells Griffin that the project will undoubtedly draw the ire of the South's militant White supremacists:

"It's a crazy idea," he said. "You'll get
yourself killed fooling around down there."
But he could not hide his enthusiasm...

Griffin, undeterred, insists that he is both aware of the precarity and also willing to incur the risk. A deal is then struck that sees *Sepia* fund Griffin's travels in the South in exchange for the right to publish excerpts from the forthcoming book.

Griffin flew to New Orleans the following week and immediately got to work on the logistics of his transformation (a mix of drugs, tanning, and stain). Once he was satisfied with his appearance, he spent six weeks traveling around the South, writing in a very personal, emotional tone about all that he encountered. Much like Sprigle's book, *Black Like Me* is structured as a series of journal entries.

The journalist familiarized himself with many facets of Southern society in a relatively short period of time. He endured the indignity of the segregated bus networks, restrooms, restaurants, and cafes. He worked as a shoe-shiner. He hitchhiked. He slept on the floor of a straggly Alabama shack with an impoverished Black couple and their six young children. He saw a wide and illuminating swath of life, interacting with nearly every archetype that existed in the Jim Crow South.

When Griffin returned to Texas and provided *Sepia's* editor with the journalistic fruits of the trip, the editor remained wary. Though he had already financed the trip, he gave Griffin another chance to avoid publication and the inevitable torrent of outrage that would follow:

> *"It'll cause trouble," he said. "We don't want to see you killed. What do you think? Hadn't we better forget the whole thing?"*

Once again, Griffin insisted that his story must see the light of day.

In late February of 1960, news of what Griffin had done broke around the country. Overnight, he became a national media figure. He was invited on the Hollywood-recorded Paul Coates show in March… then to New York City for an interview with *Time* magazine… and then a long spate of national print and television appearances. The interview with Mike Wallace, broadcast to millions from coast to coast, had a particularly transformative impact on Griffin's public profile.

Black Like Me was also a massive development internationally. Radio-Television Française, of Griffin's teenage host nation, flew a crew out to Texas for three entire days of special programming.

The public reception was not all that surprising. Griffin's project was favorably received in the nation's more progressive regions. Many Whites and Blacks alike lauded the writer for what they saw as a brave and imaginative way of steering America in a more just direction. His methodology did not offend them. His act of becoming Black did not offend them. As a potential point of controversy or moral failing, his execution of blackface didn't even occur to them. A lot of people — and certainly the majority of people who considered themselves allies of the Civil Rights Movement — celebrated *Black Like Me*. Griffin reportedly received 6,000 letters in the weeks following the book's announcement, of which only nine were abusive.

But lots of people were upset by the book, and those who were made their views known loudly and forcefully.

Perhaps the point is obvious, but I'll make it anyway: the people who *did* criticize Griffin for his book were not upset by the act of blackface, *per se*. Rather, Griffin's opponents opposed his motives, his civic ambitions. They were mad that he was upsetting the established social order of the Jim Crow South, which was rapidly shifting at the time. The status of the White man as the clear and unquestionable racial hegemon, below which all other races of American kneeled, was eroding. Anxiety and indignation were widespread amongst America's 'founding stock.'

As Griffin toured the country doing promo, and as his story gained traction in the media, his Texas-based family began to receive threatening phone calls from aggrieved neighbors. Toward the end of the book, Griffin recounts one such call:

> *"Why, he's just thrown the door wide open for those niggers, and after we've all worked so hard to keep them out." She then became abusive and succeeded in terrorizing my mother by telling her, "If you could just hear what they're planning to do to him if he ever comes back to Mansfield–"*

A local roadside cafe hung a sign in front of their building that read "WHITES ONLY", which was joined by another that read "NO ALBINOS ALLOWED", echoing the sentiment of Mansfield segregationists who viewed Griffin's work as an appalling act of racial betrayal.

In April, a mob of segregationists lynched Griffin in effigy. A dummy, painted half-white and half-black, was strung up on Mansfield's Main Street for pedestrians to observe. After a few hours had passed, the police took the dummy down and threw it on a town dump heap, from where it was promptly retrieved and then hung up on a sign that read "$25 FOR DUMPING DEAD ANIMALS".

Overwhelmed by the harassment in Mansfield, Griffin relocated his family to Dallas. The move didn't solve the problem. Despite being a much larger community, he continued to be recognized. The threats kept coming.

> ... a truck pulled up beside me and a young man in a cowboy hat looked down into the cab of my car. He told me he'd heard talk that 'they' were planning to come and castrate me, that the date had been set. He said this coldly, without emotion, neither threatening nor sympathetic, exactly the way one would say: 'The weatherman's promising rain for tomorrow.'

In August, Griffin and his family fled to Mexico in order to escape the increasingly menacing acts of harassment leveled at them by Southern Whites who were upset by the book's announcement.

After half a year in exile, Griffin returned to America for the official release of *Black Like Me*. In the years that followed the book's publication, he leveraged his newfound fame to campaign alongside such illustrious civil rights leaders as MLK and Dick Gregory. These and other voices at the forefront of the Black community embraced him. He traveled the nation extensively, delivering hundreds of public lectures on the topic of racial injustice. He was a respected voice that many Blacks and Whites alike were eager to hear.

The continued advocacy brought about continued risk, of course… Outspoken critics of Jim Crow were beaten and sometimes killed. This is a reality to which Griffin had stoically resigned himself.

And eventually the mob got to him… … …

Apart from the constant stream of threats and abuse that Griffin was subjected to, he also became the victim of a brutal physical attack. In 1964, after *Back Like Me* had become a national bestseller and Griffin a national celebrity, the 44-year-old author was tracked down by segregationists in Mississippi and violently beaten with chains. The assault took him months to recover. And yet, he didn't stop talking about race. He didn't retire. He was a soldier until the day he died in September of 1980.

Griffin was a mammoth. There are few people who had a greater impact on American race relations throughout the course of the Civil Rights Movement, and fewer still who were White. Since its release, *Black Like Me* has sold tens of millions of copies around the world. For decades, it has been on required reading lists in institutions ranging from middle schools to graduate schools. It is, by every conceivable metric, one of the most important pieces of American literature to be produced in the past hundred years.

The third doer of journalistic blackface, and to this day the only woman who has employed the tactic, was Grace Halsell. She was an American journalist and author, notable for her deep commitment to civil rights issues, evidenced by her nation-captivating travelog *Soul Sister*. Published in 1969, *Soul Sister* chronicles Halsell's transformative undercover journey into the world of Blacks in the late 1960s.[6]

For her exploration, Halsell darkened herself to pass as a Black woman, first in Harlem and then in various parts of Mississippi. Through her immersive experience, Halsell aimed to understand and document the systemic racism and daily struggles faced by Black Americans who lived through the opening innings of a post-Civil Rights Act America. Her account vividly portrays the harsh realities of prejudice, economic hardship, and social disparities that persisted from the Jim Crow era, an era that was so vividly illustrated by Sprigle and Griffin.

She documented the beginning of the liminal time between a society premised on formal discrimination and the world we know today.

Soul Sister is an engrossing read, especially for those who have read Sprigle and Griffin. It offers a firsthand look at the discrimination and challenges of the day, highlighting the enduring exposure of Blacks to racial intolerance and social segregation.

Like Sprigle and Griffin, Halsell lived as colorfully and unconventionally as any of her contemporaries. As Gore Vidal testified, "She has led the most interesting and courageous life — or lives — of any American of our time." She was a special, strong-willed woman, one who sought out Griffin's counsel in preparation for her career-defining escapade. Though multiple women had previously approached him about replicating *Black Like Me* from the female perspective, Griffin discouraged all but Halsell — Halsell, a fellow Texan, being the only woman who he believed to possess the requisite "guts" for such a project.[7]

In addition to penning *Soul Sister*, Halsell worked as a White House speech writer under President Lyndon B. Johnson, where she became the most senior woman amongst the presidential staff. Following her time at the White House, her quest to demystify societal issues through her own eyes led her to other daring projects. In her 1973 book *Bessie Yellowhair,* Halsell disguised herself as a Navajo woman to expose the exploitation of Native Americans in the domestic worker industry. She also ventured into the lives of undocumented workers from Mexico in *The Illegals*, portraying their struggles and the grim realities of crossing the border into the United States. Through these experiences and countless others — ranging from living on a fishing junk in Hong Kong, to studying at the Sorbonne in Paris, to writing for a Spanish-language paper in the Andes — Halsell's ventures underscored her commitment to chronicling human variation of every flavor, establishing her as a fearless and influential figure in immersive journalism.

The fourth act of journalistic blackface, and the first since the 1960s, took place in September of 2023.

In the dying days of last summer, I set out with a backpack of clothes, my laptop, a synthetic Afro wig, colored contact lenses, and virtually nothing else.

I was uneasy about what I was doing, but I felt I had to do it.

I felt I had no choice but to do it.

Resolved that the project was something I must complete, I flew from New York to Nashville in order to begin the two-week period of racial transformation on which the book you're reading is largely based.

I did it.

Though only for a short window, I became Black. I experienced the world as a Black man.

Hmmmm……

Is there anyone else alive who truly knows what it is like to live in both skins? Is there anyone else alive on planet earth who has done what I've done? Countless cultural figures have either publicly done or been caught in performative blackface, but they didn't *really* mean to be Black. They were doing it for a laugh. They weren't actually trying to be Black the way that Sprigle, Griffin, Halsell, and I tried to be Black.

I wonder, is there anyone but the four of us who has done it for real?

Is there anyone else alive who has experienced what I've experienced?

I don't know…

It seems that I am the first person to earnestly cross the color barrier in over half a century; the first person to do so in this millennium; the first person to do so in a post-Rodney King America; the first to do so in a post-Obama presidency America; the first to do so in a post-Trayvon Martin, post-Eric Garner, post-Michael Brown, and post-George Floyd America; and the first person to do so in myriad other ways that will be explained in the forthcoming pages.

Sprigle, Griffin, and Halsell wrote their respective books in the ways that they did because they were audacious and creative. They were unflinching in the face of danger and unfettered by the shackles of orthodoxy. They were courageous. They wanted to write books that were stimulating, challenging, relevant, and consequential.

They wanted what all writers want — they just wanted it more.

I hope that you find the vigor of their work reflected in my own.

I hope that their spirits echo posthumously in the pages that follow.

But before that, there are five notes I feel compelled to make: four about the creative decisions that went into the production of this book, and a final one that serves as a public warning.

1.

Unlike my predecessors, I did not ask for the permission of any Black person or group to write my book. Nobody gave their blessing.

Many writers would conclude that the sensible way to go about publishing something like this would be to go out and find a respectable Black journalist or academic who is willing to give a 2,000-word preamble testifying to the nobility of my character and the intellectual earnestness of the project.

After a brief bit of reflection, however, I decided that seeking out this sort or affirmation was wholly unnecessary.

Many Black individuals came to mind when I began to brainstorm suitable authors for a foreword. Black America has an incredibly rich and lively intellectual community, and there are scores of people who I would have been honored to be introduced by. These are people who I hope will engage with the book. I hope they grapple with the book's contents openly and forthrightly. I hope they find it interesting.

I hope it contributes positively to the discourse, and more generally, to America's social fabric.

With all of that being said, I am horrified by the prospect of coming off as obsequious or insincere to my readers. And I am convinced that prefacing this book with a tepidly written note from a Black person would have struck entirely the wrong tone.

2.

Relatedly, I decided against forfeiting my editorial discretion to a publisher. I decided that maintaining complete creative authority was a priority.

I actually have no clue how difficult it would have been to land a contract from a traditional publishing house for this project. Very early on in the writing process, I concluded that it likely wouldn't be worth spending the time to find out.

Perhaps some query letters would be met with interest. Perhaps there was a partner out there who would have seen the book's potential. Perhaps someone would've made the assessment that the proverbial juice was worth the squeeze. I really don't know.

This book is completely mine. It is being released by Slaughterhouse, which is a publishing company that I have recently created as a vessel for all of my writing that lacks a more suitable home.

I am the sole owner and director of Slaughterhouse. For better or worse, all decisions that went into producing this book were mine.

3.

Blackface has historically been understood as a visual phenomenon. As an act, it is evocative because it is visual. Minstrel shows were not marketed toward blind people, obviously.

And so, despite the fact that *journalistic blackface* and *minstrel blackface* are clearly very different from one another, I do feel compelled to comment on the visuals produced (or not produced) from the four aforementioned books — Sprigle's, Griffin's, Halsell's, and my own.

If images of a blackfaced Sprigle exist, I have not seen them.

Both Griffin and Halsell shared pictures of themselves in journalistic blackface as part of the promotion of their books. These images can easily be found online.

Griffin and Halsell made the decision to release images in a much different cultural context than the one that exists today. While blackface had largely died out as a form of entertainment by the 1960s, being caught in blackface was not nearly as radical a transgression of social norms as it is today. The notion of professional jeopardy for having blackface images circulating out in the world is one that I doubt ever occurred to Halsell or Griffin.

As one might expect, the notion does bother me. I am a man of my time.

Whether or not the Blacks of the 1960s were as outwardly opposed to the act of blackface as are contemporary Blacks is not clear to me. Certainly, White people have become much more outwardly offended by it. On this subject, however, it's tough to ascertain how much outrage is sincere and how much is performative. Public discourse feels drastically more contrived and strategically shaped than in previous decades. Likewise, the moral misdeeds from which people are expected to recoil feel drastically more political and specific than in previous decades.

In any case, I have decided against releasing images of myself.

The phenomenon of blackface, particularly as a feature of minstrel performances, has left an incredibly damaging mark on America. I truly believe this. I acknowledge that the painful legacy has reverberated to this day. Given the nation's dark history of racial oppression and subjugation, a history that frequently involved derogatory caricature and performance, I am sure that many Black Americans experience an instinctive psychological pain upon seeing a White person in blackface, even when the blackface is journalistic in nature.

I totally understand this. I recognize the reality of their pain. I do not want to induce it needlessly, especially when doing so offers no value to my book as a literary object.

I fully understand that even the act of putting this book out will upset many people, and if there was a way for me to magically massage away their anguish without diluting the book's substance, I would happily do it.

If you are reading this book because you are hoping to discover pictures of me lathered in greasepaint or shoe polish with cartoonishly painted lips and a toothy grin like the minstrel performers of the 1910s, you've made a mistake. You've probably made many mistakes. That's not what this is.

I'm sure the media buzz caused by images would generate significant publicity for the book — publicity that would inevitably boost sales.

But I didn't write this book to make money or to instigate a media circus.

I wrote this book in order to penetrate the tortuous and misunderstood issue of American race relations, an issue that is of the utmost importance if peace, harmony, and prosperity are to define the America of tomorrow. In addition to constituting a tremendous literary achievement, I believe that this book constitutes a tremendous achievement in the realm of civic progress.

This book is not meant to turn me into a meme, a punchline, or a pariah. I wrote it because it's the best book I felt I could write. It's the most important book I felt I could write. And to the extent that people engage with *Seven Shoulders*, they will engage with it as a book, as a collection of observations and reflections about the reality of race in America, not as photographs that can be estranged from my writing and used to stigmatize me.

4.

People may wonder why I felt it necessary to become a Black man in order to produce this book.

Couldn't you have just asked Black people about their experience? Couldn't you have simply asked them about the litany of ways in which they're discriminated against?

Many such books have been written — both by Blacks and by Whites — and most of them are tremendously boring. The fact that American Blacks have a *different* perspective than American Whites does not mean they have a *broader* perspective. A sizable swath of White America realizes this, and accordingly, there are plenty of Whites who believe that Black racial grievance is a psychological invention. They believe that it's made up, or that it's mostly made up. Griffin addressed this point at length. Many Whites are skeptical of the experiential testimony offered up by Blacks because

Blacks have never been anything but Black. And because of this, Black people have no experiential barometer with respect to race.

Nobody has an experiential barometer with respect to race, for that matter …

…

nobody except for me…

And you may say that my barometer is imperfectly calibrated. You may say that I haven't lived enough Black life for my barometer to be useful.

Say what you will.

My barometer is better than anyone else's.

5.
This last point is the most important one.

I don't know what the reaction to this book will be. I don't know how it will be handled by the media or received by the public. I don't know how the launch will change my life.

It's possible that, like Griffin, I'll be attacked.

It's possible that I'll be forced to leave the country.

I am prepared for the criticism. I am prepared for the ostracism. I am prepared for exile.

I am prepared to never land another writing job in my life.

I am prepared for *Seven Shoulders* to be my most crushing personal disaster.

But if you use this book as a pretense to attack my friends or family, if you threaten them or go at them in any way, I will do everything in my power to ruin you. I will make destroying you my rabid obsession, and I won't stop until you're either dead or so fucked up that you wish you were.

PART ONE: ON JOURNALISTIC BLACKFACE

CHAPTER 1: JUMP JIM CROW

For foreign readers who didn't learn about the Jim Crow era in grade school, and for Americans whose familiarity with the particulars have waned, it's worth reviewing just how harsh things really were.

And it's worth reviewing just how long Jim Crow lasted...

Spanning roughly the century between the Civil War and the Civil Rights Act, this period in American history saw dramatic changes in the social standing and liberty of Blacks. The position of the American Black on the day of the surrender at Appomattox was not the same as the position of the American Black on the day that LBJ took the oath of office. The difference between these points in time was massive.

For this entire period, however, and in virtually every context, Blacks were subjugated by America's White majority. In circumstances where this was not true as a matter of law, it was true as a matter of practice.

Even as recently as the immediate postwar era, the Black experience in America bore little resemblance to the one that exists today...

CHAPTER 2: WHAT SPRIGLE SAW

In the year 1948, when Sprigle visited the American South to write his book, the reality of racial oppression was marked by a complex interplay of laws, policies, and institutional practices that were designed to perpetuate Black impoverishment. Jim Crow was very much alive. Despite the Second World War's role in challenging some aspects of racial inequality, Blacks continued to face profound discrimination.

Two of the main points of cultural analysis in Sprigle's book are the institutions of tenant farming and sharecropping. I suspect that most Americans don't know the difference. The distinction between the two systems isn't widely discussed, but it's worth reflecting on if for no other reason than to demonstrate how close something can be to slavery without actually being called slavery.

Tenant farming was a system where a farmer, typically one with a little bit of their own capital, rented land from a landowner in exchange for cash rent or a portion of the crop produced on the land. Tenant farmers were renters, and they were able to leverage their small amount of economic liberty against landowners in order to secure agreements. They had some degree of control over what they planted and some degree of control over their daily activities. They could make decisions about crop management, and they had the potential to turn a profit, which could lead to greater economic stability and independence. Sometimes it could even lead to the purchase of land and the establishment of Black-owned tenant farming operations. Sprigle documents cases, though admittedly outliers, where Blacks ascended this way to become wealthy, even by White standards.

But the wealthy, landowning Black was not a common character in the Jim Crow South. The sharecropping Black was.

Sharecropping was something entirely different from tenant farming. It became widely adopted in the South during Reconstruction and lasted well into the 20th century. Under this system, landlords provided the land, tools, and seeds, while sharecroppers provided the labor. As a blunt economic matter, these laborers were little more than muscle. They would suffer through long, monotonous days in the sun, from the time it rose until the time it set. In the autumn, harvested crops were divided between landlord and sharecropper according to their agreement — typically, sharecroppers received about one-third to one-half of the harvest. As Sprigle points out, however, many Black sharecroppers did not possess the basic numeracy skills required to ensure that they received what was owed to them. Those Blacks who actually had received some sort of rudimentary training in mathematics enjoyed no safe or feasible avenue of rectifying underpayment. "Figurin' behind the man," as it was colloquially known, was not an act that White sharecroppers tolerated. The Black sharecroppers who agitated for more money faced threats, legal action, and violent physical reprisal. Recalcitrance brought beatings.

What's more, sharecroppers were often bound to the landowner by crushing volumes of personal debt, as they had to borrow against future crops to buy necessities from a landowner's store, commonly at inflated prices. Oftentimes the accounting was totally fraudulent. Again, Black sharecroppers were rarely provided with a complete and transparent tabulation of expenses. This system was notoriously exploitative. It frequently trapped sharecroppers in a cycle of debt and poverty, making it difficult for them to leave the property or achieve any sort of upward economic mobility.

These were not niche or insignificant institutions. Both systems were integral to the agricultural economy of the Jim Crow South and were heavily influenced by the totalizing racial currents and segregational laws of the time. Even if they were educated (and almost none of them were), white collar and high-paying labor jobs were not accessible to most Blacks. In the workforce, segregation was comprehensive and robust.

Blacks had a very difficult time getting hired, and an even more difficult time getting promoted. At the time, there were very few sectors outside of agriculture that Blacks were allowed to enter. At least in the South, tenant farming and sharecropping were basically the only options, with sharecropping in particular betraying the oppressive racial relations that characterized the era.

And there were no Black politicians to hail for redress...

Sprigle talks about the democratic process and the administrative mechanisms that existed in order to prevent Blacks from exercising their legal enfranchisement. He talks about how Blacks would be bullied away from the voter registry, and about how they would be bullied away from actually casting a ballot in the unlikely event that they did manage to make their way onto a voter list.

Sprigle also observes how local leaders in Southern states would sometimes let a small handful of "trusted blacks" register to vote so that lynchings could go uninterrupted — so that Southern Whites could be indemnified from the progressive legal injunctions of the Supreme Court:

> *As in every county, the white folks want a few Negroes on the registry lists from which jury talesmen are drawn. That's because when the White folks decide to 'hang a nigger' legally, by due process, with jury, judge and hangman all in order, no meddlesome 'nigger-loving' Supreme Court is going to halt the hangman because there were no Negroes eligible for jury duty.*

In the Jim Crow South, the protections promised by the 15th Amendment meant almost nothing.

Sprigle talks about the system of healthcare for Blacks — or rather, the lack thereof.

Throughout Sprigle's time, Blacks received markedly inferior care compared to their White compatriots. Hospitals were segregated by law and by practice. Facilities for Black patients went underfunded, understaffed, and often lacked in the basic medical equipment and sanitary conditions that were standard in the hospitals that served White populations. Black hospitals had fewer beds per capita, and these facilities were frequently housed in converted buildings that were ill-suited for medical treatment. Moreover, the number of trained, licensed Black physicians was disproportionately low due to barriers in medical education and licensing, further limiting access to quality healthcare for Blacks.

Even in emergencies, Jim Crow was ironclad. Sprigle documents one particularly poignant example of an expectant mother whose sudden need for a cesarean forced her to rush to the nearest "Negro hospital," situated much further away than a White hospital that possessed all of the necessary resources to deliver the child:

> Clarksdale boasts of a small but adequate
> hospital. But it is sacred to white patients.
> Dr. Hill didn't even seek admission for his
> wife and unborn baby. Just before midnight
> he put them into an ambulance and started
> a mad drive north to Memphis and its
> Negro hospital, seventy-eight miles away,
> in a desperate race with death. Death won.
> Mother and newborn baby both died on the
> operating table just before dawn.

This systemic inequality extended to preventative care and public health as well. Programs aimed at combating widespread diseases such as tuberculosis, malaria, and venereal diseases were less likely to benefit Black communities, and when they did, they were often carried out with less urgency and fewer resources. The cumulative effect of these disparities was a significant health gap between Black and White Americans, one that could be seen in mortality rates and life expectancy.

Sprigle talks about why education was so conspicuously absent from the Black community. He notes how primary education for Black children was starkly underfunded and qualitatively inferior to the institutions provided to Whites.

Schools for Black students were often makeshift structures, sometimes mere shacks, lacking basic facilities like heating, adequate lighting, and sanitary amenities. The teachers were paid less and came into the role with less education of their own. Textbooks were scarce, often hand-me-downs from White schools, worn and outdated. The educational materials and resources available were limited, and the curriculum was frequently less modern and relevant.

Bussing was rare. Students walked, and they walked far. Sprigle says that he regularly encountered children who were forced to hike six miles in order to get to their shanty schools.

Owing to economic necessity, truancy was the norm. Elementary-aged children would routinely miss months of class at a time in order to work the cotton fields for their parents' landowners. At plowin' time, plantin' time, and choppin' time, Black children were not in desks.

All of this was totally legal and rooted in law. *Plessy v. Ferguson*, decided 50 years prior, provided a legal basis for segregated schools under the doctrine of "separate but equal." As Sprigle labors to emphasize throughout the book, Jim Crow schools were as *separate* as one could possibly imagine, and also as *unequal* as one could possibly imagine.

Similarly, Sprigle talks about the fact of segregation in public accommodations. Blacks were procedurally denied access to public facilities, including restaurants, theaters, and restrooms marked "whites only." This institutionalized segregation was an inescapable reality of daily life and a totalizing symbol of racial inequality.

In the year of Sprigle's expedition, America was characterized by systemic housing discrimination that effectively segregated

Black and White populations and limited economic mobility for Blacks. One of the primary mechanisms of this discrimination was the practice of redlining, whereby maps were drawn to define areas where banks would avoid investments based on community demographics.

Predominantly Black neighborhoods were marked as high risk and were systematically denied mortgages, home improvement loans, and other financial services, thereby confining Black residents to poorer areas with substandard housing. Banks and city planners cloaked these policies in euphemisms. Given the brightness of the lines, however, it was difficult to ignore the nakedness of the racism.

Additionally, racially restrictive covenants were common in property deeds. These covenants were agreements embedded into the deed of a property that prohibited the sale or rental of the property to individuals of specific races — often Black people. This practice ensured that affluent neighborhoods remained virtually all White, barring Black families from accessing better amenities and the schools associated with these areas.

Local zoning laws also contributed to the segregation, relegating Black communities to less desirable parts of towns and cities — near industrial areas or waste disposal sites, for example. These laws degraded Black quality of life and also the value of Black properties, perpetuating a cycle of poverty that limited capital accumulation. Financially, it was suffocating.

Such institutional barriers were deeply entrenched, ensuring racial segregation was firmly maintained — socially, economically, and as a blunt matter of urban geography.

Sprigle talks about the nature of criminal justice in the Jim Crow South too.

At the time Sprigle was writing, the criminal justice system in the Southern states was characterized by dramatic racial disparities in law enforcement, judicial proceedings, and punishment. Laws were disproportionately enforced against Blacks, often targeting them with vagrancy statutes and other petty offenses that were seldom applied to Whites. "Pig Laws," for instance, disproportionately penalized petty thefts related to livestock with severe sentences, and these laws were disproportionately applied to Blacks.

The adjudication process for Blacks accused of crimes was frequently marred by bias. Many Blacks faced all-White juries that were prone to convict based on racial prejudice rather than evidence. Legal defense for Blacks was inadequate, often provided by underfunded and overworked public defenders who lacked the resources to offer effective representation. This lack of fair trial opportunities proved a significant obstacle to many Blacks facing criminal charges, whether the charges were legitimate or baseless.

There were almost no Black people on police forces when Sprigle was writing. On this matter, tides were beginning to turn as the '50s approached, but only at a glacial pace. Sprigle recalls observing the first group of Black policemen to serve in Atlanta: they were not able to arrest Whites, they were not permitted to carry guns, and they were forced to police only the most violent parts of the city.

Punishments were typically harsher for Blacks compared to their White counterparts. Sentences were more severe, and conditions in prisons were particularly brutal for Black inmates. Additionally, the enforcement of the death penalty was notably disproportionate. Rape allegations, particularly those involving Black men accused of raping White women, led to death sentences, whereas similar cases with reversed racial roles resulted in lesser penalties, if they were penalized at all.

Sprigle talks about chain gangs, a notoriously harsh punishment regime wherein Blacks, often convicted of minor offenses, were forced to perform hard labor in public, chained together for control and humiliation. These gangs primarily worked on infrastructure projects like building roads, clearing land, or digging ditches, under extremely brutal and tiring conditions. The offenses that could lead to such severe punishment were frequently trivial — such as loitering, small thefts, or other minor infractions — yet the sentences were disproportionately harsh as a means of continuing racial control and providing a glut of cheap labor.

The individuals in chain gangs endured long hours of physically exhausting work, inadequate food and shelter, and often inhumane treatment from guards. It reified the social order of White supremacy by dehumanizing Black individuals and subjecting them to public degradation.

Sprigle talks about the ominous, and universally understood phenomenon of "the word."

In the Jim Crow South, "the word" referred to a menacing, ambiguous threat used to enforce racial hierarchy and control the behavior of Blacks, particularly Black men. This term encapsulated the unwritten rule that any Black individual who contravened established social norms — or who in any way upset or challenged a White person — could expect retribution. The specific nature of the word was deliberately vague, but it implied severe consequences, including the pain of physical violence, lynching, or other fatal forms of extrajudicial punishment.

This form of social control was a powerful and coercive tool in maintaining the racial order. For instance, if a Black man failed to yield the sidewalk to a White passerby, made eye contact with a White woman in a manner deemed inappropriate, or disputed a White man's testimony, he could be given the word. The threat hung in the air, and entire communities were aware of it.

The word was all-encompassing. It was part of a broader system of oppression that included economic, legal, and physical threats to enforce subservience and compliance from the Black community. It served as a constant, looming reminder that deviation from the subordinate role prescribed to

Blacks could, and often did, result in swift and brutal retribution. This informal enforcement mechanism worked alongside more formal, explicit Jim Crow laws and policies to sustain a deeply segregated and comprehensively unequal society.

Sprigle saw and documented all of these facets of Jim Crow, the ones that kept Blacks from fully engaging with all of the primary institutions of civic life.

He also took note of Jim Crow's less infamous manifestations.

He noted the frequency with which Blacks were refused car insurance on the grounds that Whites would not believe their testimony in court. In collisions between Blacks and Whites, Black drivers were deemed at fault as a matter of course.

He noted the Whites-only beaches, the construction and maintenance of which were funded by taxes from both Blacks and Whites. In particular, he recalls the story of a Black domestic worker who eventually protests against her White boss after being forced to bathe the White woman's mangy dog at a segregated beach:

> *"I don't think it's right," she tearfully told her mistress, "that I have to take that dog swimming every day, and if I tried to go in myself I'd be arrested. And that dog's got mange and I haven't."*

Access to drugstore fountains was a big issue. At drugstores that stocked paper cups, Blacks would be allowed a drink of water. At drugstores that only had glass cups, Blacks were not allowed to drink, not even on the hottest days — lest Black lips permanently contaminate vessels that would subsequently be used by Whites. No amount of washing could conceivably decontaminate the stain of Black lips. That was the conventional wisdom.

Sprigle documented an extremely wide array of situations where Blacks, by virtue of their inferior position in America's racial hierarchy, were treated in ways that would be seen as horrifying and unacceptable today.

Racism percolated throughout every domain of life. Jim Crow laws, which were widely popular, enforced racial segregation in the Southern United States across public spaces and in virtually every area of private life. These laws created a firm legal framework for systemic discrimination, disenfranchisement, and unrecognizably different racial experiences.

If you received a decent high school civics education, you know all of this stuff already. Please forgive the banalities. I know the reiteration is boring. Still, given the nature of what I'm doing, it does feel necessary…

I won't be lectured about Jim Crow, as if its character or scale have gone over my head.

I won't have people alleging that I fail to realize what things were like in the century of my birth. I know what happened….

Sprigle claims that the world of Jim Crow he observed was "not quite slavery, but not quite freedom." I suspect that anyone who reads his book will be left with the clinging impression that the Blacks who he walked amongst were much less like freemen than like slaves. Nothing about their lives was free.

CHAPTER 3: WHAT GRIFFIN SAW

Some of the changes that occurred in the decade between *In the Land of Jim Crow* and *Black Like Me* were significant, but they weren't *that* significant. 65 years of hindsight isn't *that* different from 75 years of hindsight.

Between the 1948 writing of *In the Land of Jim Crow* and the 1959 writing of *Black Like Me*, the United States witnessed several pivotal advances in the realm of civil rights that signaled shifts toward greater equality, albeit gradually. In 1948, President Truman ordered the desegregation of the military with Executive Order 9981, marking a significant federal move away from racial discrimination. This period also saw the Supreme Court's 1954 landmark decision in *Brown v. Board of Education*, which declared state laws establishing separate public schools for Black and White students to be unconstitutional, effectively nullifying the shaky "separate but equal" doctrine established by *Plessy v. Ferguson*. Moreover, the Montgomery Bus Boycott of 1955-1956, sparked by Rosa Parks' refusal to give up her seat to a White man, catalyzed the broader Civil Rights Movement and propelled MLK into national prominence as a figure at the vanguard of the intensifying fight for racial equality.

Despite these achievements, and when viewed within the broader arc of American history, the changes realized during this period were relatively modest. The legal and cultural structures that supported racial inequality remained deeply entrenched, and the efforts from the 11-year gap between the first and second acts of journalistic blackface, while notable, only began to scratch the surface of the pervasive and systemic nature of racial discrimination.

What Griffin saw, on a trip that was similar in scope and duration to Sprigle's, was a Jim Crow South that was only slightly closer to the America we know today.

Lynchings still took place. In particular, the recent and gruesome case of Mack Parker is one that Griffin grew familiar with during the opening days of his transracial journey.

Mack Charles Parker was a Southern Black whose 1959 lynching became the subject of widespread media attention — due to the details of the lynching itself, but also due to the fruitless criminal proceedings that followed.

Parker was accused of raping a white woman in Pearl River County, Mississippi, although there were considerable doubts amongst the relevant witnesses about the validity of the accusation. Mere days before his trial was scheduled, a mob of White men abducted Parker from his jail cell in the Pearl River County Courthouse. They beat him brutally and then shot him to death. His body was found floating in the Pearl River weeks later. Despite the public nature of the crime and substantial evidence, which included damning eyewitness accounts, no one was ever indicted. The killers walked. Griffin recalls being in Louisiana, as a Black man surrounded by other Black men, when the news of the acquittal hit the streets of New Orleans. He recalls people learning of the decision not to convict any of the White suspects, as reported in the pages of *The Louisiana Weekly*. He describes how woeful and defeating it was for the Black community to see one of their own killed, brazenly, and with total impunity: "Not since I was in Europe, when the Russo-German Pact of 1939 was signed, had I seen news spread such bitterness and despair." To be clear, though, Griffin follows this anecdote with a lengthy clarification that the verdict did not come as a surprise. Everyone knew what the outcome would be.

The segregation of public facilities was still very much in effect when Griffin toured the South. Like Sprigle, he could not eat, drink, walk, sit, or sleep, amongst the Whites. Even as progressive court rulings altered the region's legal regime, centuries of cultural inertia meant that the implementation was delayed. *De facto*, institutions in the South remained 'separate but equal.'

These major forms of institutional racism — in restaurants, in bars, in hotels, and on all forms of public transit — have been recounted *ad nauseam* in America's canon of historical literature. Personally, I find the less well-known examples more interesting and revealing of the psychology that perpetuated Jim Crow…

On a bus ride from Louisiana to Mississippi, Griffin has a conversation with a group of Southern Blacks that illustrates what I mean. One of the Blacks, while delivering a lecture on the social dictates of the South, warns Griffin against making eye contact with White women. But not only does he warn Griffin against making eye contact with real, living White women, he also admonishes him against looking at the White women who are featured on billboards and promotional posters for movies. "Hey, boy — what are you looking at that white gal like that for?" or some similarly menacing remark would be made by indignant Whites, according to Griffin's fellow passengers, seemingly speaking from experience.

Griffin notes how, on that same bus trip, he was denied the opportunity to use the bathroom during a break at a roadside rest stop, even though the stop did have a designated bathroom for Blacks. The White bus driver, Griffin recounts, did not want to risk the trouble of having to round up the Blacks when the time came to get back on the road. And so, Griffin and the other Blacks were forced to hold it. Similarly petty demonstrations of racial power are peppered throughout *Black Like Me*.

And then there was the "hate stare," a burning gaze that Griffin reports experiencing everywhere he went as a Black man. The hate stare, Griffin testifies, was a powerful and unnerving form of non-verbal aggression, one that he had never experienced in his life as a White man. It was an intense, prolonged glare directed at him, a Black man, that he instantly knew was meant to convey hostility and intimidation. Griffin notes that the hate stare served as a silent but clear message of racial contempt and a reminder of the societal boundaries that were not to be crossed by Blacks. He characterizes the phenomenon as one of the principal weapons in the arsenal used by segregationists to maintain racial hierarchy, deeply impacting the psyche of those subjected to it, vividly illustrating the pervasive nature of racism in even the most subtle forms of contact.

CHAPTER 4: WHAT HALSELL SAW

The changes that occurred between *Black Like Me* ('61) and *Soul Sister* ('69) were more substantial than the changes that occurred between *In the Land of Jim Crow* ('49) and *Black Like Me*.

Between 1961 and 1969, the American Civil Rights Movement achieved a series of dramatic milestones that markedly advanced the rights of Black Americans, catalyzing sweeping changes from coast to coast.

The period was initiated by the Freedom Rides in 1961, sponsored by the Congress of Racial Equality (CORE). The interracial activists involved in this protest challenged the segregationist status quo by traveling together on buses into the heart of the Deep South. Their goal in doing so was to enforce Supreme Court rulings that declared segregated facilities for interstate passengers unconstitutional. Despite often violent opposition, these rides drew national attention and forced federal action to protect and enforce civil rights. They pushed states and localities to obey DC.

The year 1963 marked another critical juncture when more than a quarter of a million people participated in the March on Washington for Jobs and Freedom, making it one of the largest political rallies for human rights in United States history. Here, Dr. Martin Luther King Jr. delivered his iconic "I Have a Dream" speech, which has since become one of the most emblematic cultural products of the Civil Rights Movement. This mass gathering proved critical in galvanizing support for major legislative changes, leading directly to the passage of the Civil Rights Act of 1964 — comprehensive legislation that outlawed discrimination based on race, color, religion, sex, or national origin. It also shattered the legal basis for unequal application of voter registration requirements and racial segregation in schools, workplaces, and public accommodations.

The wave of civil rights legislation continued with the Voting Rights Act of 1965, a pivotal law that struck down barriers to Black enfranchisement, particularly in the Southern states. It suspended the use of literacy tests and other discriminatory practices that had previously been used to disenfranchise Black voters.

Following the gruesome assassination of MLK in 1968, Congress passed the Fair Housing Act, which aimed to eliminate discrimination in the sale, rental, and financing of housing based on race, religion, national origin, or sex, and made it a federal crime to injure, intimidate, or interfere with anyone by reason of their race, color, religion, or national origin.

These legislative victories, hard-fought through relentless protests, advocacy, and strategic battles in both the nation's streets and Washington's corridors of power, marked a transformative decade in American history. The end of the 1960s brought slivers of the racial era we are living in today. Halsell saw the slivers, and she also saw the phenomena that existed between them…

Throughout the course of her research, Halsell lived in various Black communities, including Harlem and a string of smaller cities throughout the state of Mississippi. During her foray into the world of Black America, Halsell observed not only the external adversities but also the internal coping mechanisms of the Black community, including the strength found in familial bonds and communal support. Despite the racially oppressive environment, she conveys a resilience and a persistent hope for a better future among the people she meets. Her observations show the complex relationship of race, identity, and social structures in a nation roiled by progression and cultural turbulence.

Soul Sister's dust jacket description is well-worded:

A woman walks down the streets of Harlem — past the dilapidated houses and broken, jagged liquor bottles; past the hustlers, crap shooters, addicts, and pushers; past the kids and old men idling on the fire escapes or sitting on garbage cans. The woman's skin is black, but her memories, her fears, and her prejudices are those of a white woman. Harlem is alien territory, and as she scours the area for a rooming house or hotel room, with only twenty dollars in her purse, there is terror in her heart. Grace Halsell — a white Southern woman whose ancestors owned slaves — is the first white woman to pass as black.

She sees a lot in the book…

Halsell writes about being called a "stupid black bitch" by a New York City cab driver who she asked for a ride to Harlem. Like many Whites at the time, the cabbie characterized Harlem as a "hell-hole" and regarded it as more akin to a foreign country than to an American neighborhood merely with a darker average skin tone.

Halsell writes about the predatory commercial lending practices that targeted the Black customers at New York City department stores. Nearly everything was put on credit, with total prices routinely obscured and inflated far beyond what they would be in White neighborhoods. These portions of the book are strikingly reminiscent of Sprigle's sharecropper findings.

In a similar vein, Halsell writes about how much more expensive and less varied the groceries are in Harlem. All basic staples ranging from produce to meat to eggs cost more, if they are available at all. The term "food desert" was decades away from popularity, but that phenomenon is very much what she describes. Anyone who has had to live and feed themselves in the Black parts of New York City in recent years, as indeed I have, will find her observations especially poignant. They feel painfully timeless.

Halsell writes about the Black youth of Harlem who associate with the Black Panther movement, and who resent the older generation of middle-class Blacks for adopting bourgeois, 'White' sensibilities. This new generation often viewed their parents, especially those who had gained a degree of upward mobility, as the playthings of liberal Whites. They viewed their parents as meek…. as culturally lethargic… as insufficiently Black.

This younger generation, though, also struggled with its own co-optation, one that became the subject of intense controversy amongst New York's intelligentsia the year following *Soul Sister*'s publication, when Tom Wolfe penned his famous article about a paradoxical dinner party that tabled Black Power militants across from the most culturally influential residents of Park Avenue. *Radical chic*, as Wolfe coined this voguish political alliance, was all the rage.

It was a time of intense flux and apprehension, and Halsell was at the epicenter: East 125th and Seventh.

During her months in Mississippi, Halsell describes the *de facto* segregation of transit facilities that continued up to the twilight of the '60s despite its *de jure* disallowance at the decade's outset. She describes being aggressively targeted with epithets before being denied a room at a White boarding house. Most evocatively of all, she describes her own sexual assault, one performed by the husband of a White woman who had hired her to perform domestic labor.

She writes about a lot… … … at a very fluid and consequential point in America's adolescence.

Thanks to the decade that preceded *Soul Sister*, comprehensive civil rights protections were either legally active or in the implementation stage as she wrote, but the observable facts of the Black experience often failed to reflect this progress. An obvious lag separated legislative advances from reality.

Halsell, the glass-ceiling-shattering Texan, did an impressive job of explaining what things were like in this liminal stage — in the dying days of Jim Crow, on the verge of racial modernity.

CHAPTER 5: '69 TO OBAMA

From 1969 to the election of Barack Obama in 2008, America experienced radical changes in race relations that fundamentally remolded the Black experience.

The modern system of affirmative action in education was born during this period. For the first time in American history, Blacks were not only permitted to attend the same educational institutions as Whites, they were also proactively incentivized.

This period witnessed significant legislative developments, such as the Equal Employment Opportunity Act of 1972, which granted expansive enforcement measures to the newly formed Equal Employment Opportunity Commission. As a result, employers across the nation were increasingly subjected to ramifications for discriminatory conduct in the workplace, thereby giving teeth and bite force to the 1964 Civil Rights Act.

The Supreme Court's 1971 decision in *Swann v. Charlotte-Mecklenburg Board of Education* marked a pivotal moment in the racial politics of the American education system. It betrayed, quite controversially, the shifting sentiments of the 1970s towards more aggressive measures for desegregation. This landmark ruling authorized the use of busing as a tool to achieve integration in public schools, endorsing it as a necessary and constitutional means to dismantle the legacy of segregation. The decision came at a time when many White communities resisted integration efforts, but the Court's stance underscored a national commitment to enforce *Brown v. Board of Education* more fully. *Swann v. Charlotte-Mecklenburg* did not merely accelerate change in the racial composition of schools, but also symbolized the broader societal shift towards embracing federal intervention as essential in correcting deep-seated racial inequalities.

The *Bakke* decision of 1978 represented a significant crossroad in American civil rights and educational policy, mirroring the serpentine social trends of the 1970s. In *Regents of the University of California v. Bakke*, the Supreme Court struck down the use of rigid racial quotas in university admissions, but simultaneously upheld the constitutionality of affirmative action, acknowledging that race could be one of several factors in the admissions process. This nuanced decision highlighted the evolving societal understanding that sought to reconcile the need for remedial measures to address historic racial disparities with a growing push against policies perceived as "reverse discrimination" or "reverse racism." Many Whites were indignant, and loudly so. This ruling bookended a decade-long drama marked by intense debates over equality, diversity, and individual rights. Perhaps more than any other case, it encapsulated the era's struggle to define fairness in a society seeking both racial equality and Kingian colorblindness.

The evolution continued. In 1987, The Civil Rights Restoration Act became a significant legislative response to Supreme Court decisions that had narrowed the scope of civil rights protections. This Act, passed despite President Ronald Reagan's veto, expanded the definition of "programs or activities" receiving federal financial assistance to include entire institutions or agencies, rather than just the specific program or department receiving federal funds. This broader application meant that if any part of an institution received federal funding, the entire institution was forced to comply with existing civil rights legislation, which meant reinstating and bolstering nondiscrimination requirements across a wide range of areas — education, employment, and healthcare, most significantly. The societal ramifications were tremendous, ensuring more comprehensive enforcement of civil rights protections and reaffirming Washington's commitment to preventing discrimination on the basis of race, color, national origin, sex, or disability across all federally funded entities. This buttressed the accountability of institutions benefiting from federal support to uphold civil rights standards, significantly neutralizing public and private sector practices.

The 1992 Rodney King riots, ignited by the acquittal of four Los Angeles Police Department officers who were videotaped beating Rodney King, a Black motorist, showed the strained relations between law enforcement and the Black community. LA flew off the hinges like no American city had flown off the hinges before. The rioting, which resulted in thousands of arrests, thousands of damaged buildings, and over 50 deaths, demonstrated longstanding grievances regarding police brutality and racial disparities in the criminal justice system.

The widespread broadcast of the King beating and the violent fallout from the trial verdict brought these issues to the forefront of the national consciousness, prompting public and political discourse on a scale previously unknown. It was, in hindsight, an extremely vivid premonition of things to come. It amplified scrutiny of police conduct, particularly in interactions with Blacks, and spurred demands for reform that echoed into the following decades.... ... ... Boomingly so.

Between 1969 and 2008, the political landscape of the United States underwent sweeping, substantial changes. Clearly. There was a tectonic increase in the number of Blacks ascending to political office across various levels of government. This shift was reflective of a broader societal movement towards inclusivity and diversity within political institutions. In 1967, Carl Stokes became the first Black mayor of a major U.S. city, Cleveland, Ohio, heralding a new era of Black leadership in urban centers. This was followed by the election of Thomas Bradley as the mayor of Los Angeles in 1973, who served for an unprecedented five terms and indelibly shaped the city's development and policies.

At the federal level, the period saw Shirley Chisholm make history in 1968 as the first Black woman elected to the United States Congress, then as the first major-party Black candidate for President of the United States, and also the first woman to run for the Democratic presidential nomination in 1972.

The 1990s and 2000s, likewise, saw an increasing number of Blacks in Congress, including the influential roles played by representatives like John Lewis and senators like Carol Moseley Braun, who became the first Black woman elected to the U.S. Senate in 1992. The political ascension and election of Barack Obama as the first Black president symbolized what was, without a doubt, the most dramatic turn in the nation's racial politics…

These developments indicated a profound departure from the past, showing a country that was moving toward greater inclusivity and representation of Blacks at all levels of society — not as rapidly as many would have liked, but undeniably nevertheless.

CHAPTER 6: OBAMA TO SEVEN SHOULDERS

The past couple decades have not been so... *linear...*

Though it's difficult to say with any degree of certainty that Black people are better off in America now than they were 15 years ago, it's obvious that the current state of race relations has been profoundly influenced by the developments of the recent past, particularly since the end of the aughts.

The election of Barack Obama as President in 2008 signified a major shift in American race relations — in a way that was blindingly symbolic, if not always practical. For many, it was the thing that was never going to happen... that happened.

Obama, the son of an African man, had risen to the highest office in the United States. On paper, he was the most powerful man in the world. His victory shattered a racial barrier, but it also showed a broad, cross-racial coalition that suggested a readiness among a significant portion of the American populace to accept Black leadership.

During his tenure in the Oval Office, Obama took numerous steps to address what his administration considered to be the surviving forms of institutional racism.

Under his administration, the EEOC aggressively pursued cases of anti-Black racial discrimination. Obama's Department of Education, similarly, worked to reduce anti-Black discrimination on campuses. Support for historically Black colleges and universities was another clear priority, with Obama's administration consistently boosting funding.

In a similar manner, the Obama administration was a strong advocate for affirmative action in higher education. The Department of Justice and the Department of Education issued guidance to colleges and universities on how they could legally consider race to promote diversity, reinforcing policies that supported affirmative action in admissions processes.

Although not directly an affirmative action policy, the Fair Sentencing Act signed by Obama helped reduce racial disparities that stemmed from drug charges. This law closed the gap between sentences for crack and powder cocaine possession, which, historically, have disproportionately affected Black communities.

The Obama administration filed amicus briefs supporting the University of Texas at Austin's affirmative action admissions policy, which was challenged and ascended to the Supreme Court as *Fisher* v. *University of Texas at Austin*. The administration's firm stance was that diversity in higher education is a vital interest of the United States, and it ran the country accordingly.

Moreover, the Obama White House endeavored to support minority-owned businesses through various federal programs. The Minority Business Development Agency was strengthened to provide more support and resources to Black entrepreneurs.

For predictable reasons, the Obama presidency brought racial issues into a new focus in the public and political discourse, providing visibility to challenges and initiating discussions about racial equity on a national level. Class-based policy initiatives such as the Affordable Care Act were often formulated and sold to the Black community as a genre of racial reparations. And his base embraced these moves as a win for Blacks, largely because of his cultural cachet amongst the demographic…

His presence and his family's portrayal in the media challenged stereotypes and provided a powerful counter-narrative to historic representations of Blacks in America. Both the President and the First Lady were routinely emblazoned on the cover of magazines. They were lionized by the nation's establishment outlets. For the better part of a decade, they were the foremost darlings of the coastal tastemakers. During that time, the symbolic and practical impacts of Obama's presidency significantly influenced the nation's racial discourse, prompting many Americans to be optimistic about the potential for progress in racial cohesion and integration.

But hope and the promise of unity were largely phenomena of the first term. By the second term, those buoyant sentiments were exposed as sanguine naivety. By the second term, many of the people who subscribed to the "Yes we can" mantra were beginning to doubt.

Many people realized that colorblindness and racial harmony weren't just going to spontaneously appear because of the president's skin tone. The conflict of past generations was not entirely fading away. Race wasn't vanishing as a salient social issue.... ... ... And actually, race became a bigger issue in America during the second term. As a consequence, race relations deteriorated.

They deteriorated a lot... in ways that are difficult to overstate given the benefit of hindsight.

The birth of America's most influential racial movement coincided with the start of Obama's second term...

Black Lives Matter was formed in 2013 following the acquittal of George Zimmerman in the shooting death of Trayvon Martin. Founded by Alicia Garza, Patrisse Cullors, and Opal Tometi, BLM began as a hashtag on social media and evolved into a decentralized movement dedicated to protesting perceived cases of institutional racism and violence inflicted on Black communities by the state and vigilantes. The organization gained momentum with the subsequent deaths of other Black men, which were framed as further evidence of the movement's central message about police brutality. BLM's prominence grew through grassroots activism and public demonstrations, all the while demanding urgent societal and criminal justice reform.

The rise of BLM led to considerable polarization in American society. Supporters saw the movement as a vital and urgent call for change, spotlighting racial inequalities that they believed were long-ignored evidence of racial injustice.

Critics, however, contested the movement's central claim: that Black men were being systematically murdered by the nation's law enforcement without consequence. Critics also argued that BLM's approaches were too confrontational and divisive, sometimes interpreting the slogan "Black lives matter" as an implication that other lives did not. This dichotomy fostered intense debates over race, policing, and justice throughout the country. The organization's impact on public discourse around these topics made it a subject of fierce contention, reflecting and amplifying existing racial and political divides.

Ferguson was a critical flashpoint. The unrest erupted following the fatal shooting of Michael Brown, an 18-year-old Black man, by a white police officer, Darren Wilson, in the previously sleepy Missouri city of 20,000 people. The incident, which occurred in August of 2014, ignited weeks of protests, both peaceful and violent, that drew national and international attention. As had been the case countless times throughout history, America's Black-White racial drama became the axis on which everything else spun.

The protests were fueled by abiding grievances over racial profiling, police brutality, and a criminal justice system perceived as biased against Blacks. The situation in Ferguson accentuated the strained relationships between law enforcement and Black communities, particularly in areas with high poverty and racially segregated neighborhoods.

The response to the unrest involved a heavily militarized police presence, which was widely criticized and depicted in media reports as exacerbating the tension. This, in turn, led to broader discussions about the militarization of police forces across the United States.

Opportunities for racial division continued to emerge … … …

One especially disturbing case was the Charleston church shooting of 2015, a devastating, high-profile act of racially motivated violence that took place on June 17th, when a White gunman entered the Emanuel African Methodist Episcopal Church in Charleston, South Carolina, and killed nine Black churchgoers. This historic church, known for its deep roots in the Black community and its role in the Civil Rights Movement, was specifically targeted, making the attack that much more traumatic. The shooter, who had expressed White supremacist beliefs and was pictured holding Confederate flags in photos discovered post-attack, was bent on sparking a racial war.

The massacre horrified the nation and led to another intense, inflammatory discourse on race relations, hate crimes, and the enduring legacy of racism in the United States. It also reignited debates over the symbolism of the Confederate flag, which the shooter revered as a symbol of White supremacy. In response to the shooting, and amidst widespread public outcry, several state governments and businesses moved to banish or remove the Confederate flag from public display, identifying its association with racial oppression and violence... ... ...

So much stuff happened in this era. I am trying hard to only hit the most culturally germane moments... ... ...

The kneeling saga was important insofar as it preserved the initial BLM energy through the early Trump years...

The National Anthem NFL protests began in 2016 when San Francisco 49ers quarterback Colin Kaepernick knelt during the national anthem to draw attention to what he perceived to be racial injustice and police brutality against American Blacks. The gesture, which Kaepernick characterized as a necessary form of peaceful protest, quickly spread across the league. Many other (mostly Black) players joined in solidarity.

The protests ignited a nationwide debate, reflecting and ossifying Red-Blue divisions. Pro-Kaepernick Americans insisted that the athletes were exercising their right to free speech and shining light on significant injustices. Critics, however, claimed the protests were an affront to the flag and to military personnel. The controversy reached the highest levels of public discourse, with significant media coverage and even commentary from political figures, including the newly elected President, who expressed strong opposition:

> *Wouldn't you love to see one of these NFL owners, when somebody disrespects our flag, to say, "Get that son of a bitch off the field right now! Out! He's fired! He's fired!"?*

Numerous players participating in the protest, incidentally, cited Trump's election as a motivation for kneeling.[8]

During the late 2010s, there was a notable increase in the visibility and media coverage of alt-right and White nationalist groups in America. This rise was characterized by more frequent reporting of rallies, demonstrations, and online activities that included overtly racial and nationalistic rhetoric. The increased prominence of these groups was spotlit dramatically during events like the 2017 "Unite the Right" rally in Charlottesville, Virginia, which ended in violence and the declaration of a state of emergency by Governor Terry McAuliffe. The visibility of such groups stirred significant unease among Blacks and other minorities, some of whom perceived the developments as a direct threat to their safety and civil rights. The public nature of these groups' activities led to heightened fears of emboldened racial hostility. This resurgence of White nationalist visibility prompted calls for stronger responses from civic leaders and lawmakers to address and counteract White identitarian movements, with Democrats, predictably, making the issue a more central focus than Republicans.

The election of Donald Trump in 2016, relatedly, was perceived by many on the American left as a regressive shift in the nation's approach to issues affecting the Black community. This perception was influenced by Trump's rhetoric and policy proposals, which some critics argued could undermine civil rights gains and promote divisive attitudes. The administration's rhetorical posture on policing, affirmative action, and immigration, among other issues, contributed to a sense of unease and frustration within segments of the Black community and among allied liberal factions consumed by the topic of racial justice. These sentiments were further fueled by the administration's somewhat equivocal statements on issues of racial identitarianism, leading to heightened anxiety about the future direction of civil rights policies. Despite Donald Trump's repeated efforts to brand himself as a leader for the Black community, the administration's public image led to widespread debate and discussions about the impact of federal policies on racial disparities and the broader social climate in the United States.

And then there was Covid, which marked the beginning of where we are now. Covid was the intro to the current moment... ... ...

The COVID-19 pandemic brought to the surface profound racial health disparities within the United States. Study after study revealed that Blacks experienced disproportionately high rates of infection, severe illness, and mortality compared to Whites. Several factors contributed to this disparity, including higher prevalence of pre-existing conditions such as hypertension and diabetes, which are more common amongst American Blacks.

The economic effects, too, were disproportionate, as Black communities suffered greater job losses and financial instability throughout the pandemic, further exposing historic inequalities in access to healthcare and economic opportunities.[9] COVID-19 brought these issues into sharper focus. It revived discussions on how to address systemic inequalities effectively — in university classes, in corporate boardrooms, in government offices, in basically all realms of American life. It was a fraught, foreboding time... ... ...

The '20s, this new and modern decade, started out with a cataclysmic public health event that was racialized from the beginning... ... ...

And the racialization soon escalated with another cataclysm.

~~...~~ because **HE** ~~overdosed was strangled was murdered~~ ... died ...

Yes, the summer of 2020 was the Summer of Floyd... the summer of the video... and the coroner's report... and the crowds... and the black squares... and the rallies... and the riots... and the fires... the summer that everything happened... the summer that everything changed... ... ...

In some ways, it feels like 2024 is year four in the world of race relations. It does feel like that summer is the genesis of the racial world we live in today. And it is not much of an exaggeration to say that Floyd's posthumous treatment has often verged on Christ-like veneration. In the eyes of many, he was a martyr — a tragic and heroic victim of America's undying commitment to White supremacy.

The death of George Floyd on May 25th, 2020, was the most significant turning point in American race relations in the modern era.

I will try to render as descriptive an accounting of the Floyd incident and its aftermath as I can:

George Floyd, a 46-year-old Black man, died after a physical altercation took place during his arrest in Minneapolis, Minnesota. During the course of his arrest, Floyd was restrained by Derek Chauvin (a White police officer) in a controversial physical hold for over nine minutes while being handcuffed and positioned face down on the street.

The specifics of the incident, including Floyd's significant fentanyl and methamphetamine intoxication, were not publicly known, and it was widely believed at the time that Floyd's death was the cause of Chauvin's actions. Furthermore, and relatedly, it was widely believed that Chauvin's actions were caused by racial animosity.

This graphic incident — which was captured on video and quickly disseminated across media and social networks — sparked a massive and widespread protest movement across the United States under the banner of Black Lives Matter. All of this happened in a matter of hours from the time of Floyd's death, and all of it was framed as a fundamentally racial incident from the start.

The emotional public reaction forced American commentators to return to the thorny, longstanding issues of perceived police brutality and racial inequality in the criminal justice system. Cities nationwide saw continuous demonstrations, some of which became incredibly destructive. In Minneapolis, the movement's focal point, hundreds of buildings were burned. Stores were looted. Neighborhoods were destroyed. For weeks, mass demonstrations were held in every major city throughout the country, and even in a handful of cities abroad.

In response to Floyd's death, there was a significant mobilization within both government and corporate sectors across the United States to address racial inequalities. Various governmental bodies at the local, state, and federal levels initiated discussions and began implementing policy reforms aimed at policing and criminal justice system overhauls.

Some of the displays of solidarity performed by elected officials were extremely dramatic... ... ...

Nancy Pelosi, arguably the most powerful woman in the world, framed Floyd's death as tantamount to the assassination of MLK or Robert Kennedy:

> *Thank you, George Floyd, for sacrificing your life for justice, for being there to call out to your mom… But because of you, and because of thousands, millions of people around the world who came out for justice, your name will always be synonymous with justice.*

Pelosi, flanked by a squadron of Democratic colleagues, also drew attention for kneeling in a moment of memorial silence while wearing Kente cloth, a traditional African sash.

Joe Biden's statement on Floyd's death is illuminating as well. It provides insight into the psychology and racial attitudes of the millions of Americans who would vote him into office later that year:

Once again — the words "I can't breathe."

An act of brutality so elemental, it did more than deny one more black man in America his civil rights and his human rights. It denied his very humanity. It denied him of his life.

Depriving George Floyd — as it deprived Eric Garner — of the one thing every human being must be able to do: Breathe.

So simple. So basic. So brutal.

The same thing happened with Ahmaud Arbery. The same with Breonna Taylor. The same thing with George Floyd.

We've spoken their names aloud. Cried them out in pain and horror. Chiseled them into long-suffering hearts.

They are the latest additions to an endless list of lives stolen — potential wiped out unnecessarily.

It's a list that dates back more than 400 years: black men, black women, black children.

The original sin of this country still stains our nation today. Sometimes we manage to overlook it, and just push forward with the thousand other tasks of daily life. But it's always there.

And weeks like this, we see it plainly.

We are a country with an open wound.

None of us can turn away. None of us can be silent.

None of us any longer can hear those words — "I can't breathe" — and do nothing.

We cannot fall victim to what Martin Luther King called the "appalling silence of the good people."

Every day, African Americans go about their lives with constant anxiety and trauma, wondering — who will be next?

Imagine if every time your husband or son, wife or daughter, left the house, you feared for their safety from bad actors and bad police.

Imagine if you had to have that talk with your child about not asserting their rights — and taking the abuse handed out to them — just so they could make it home.

Imagine having the police called on you — for just sitting in Starbucks or renting an Airbnb or watching birds.

That is the norm for black people in this nation — they don't have to imagine it.

The anger and the frustration and the exhaustion — it's undeniable. But that is not the promise of America.

And it is long past time we made the promise of this nation real for all people.

This is no time for incendiary tweets. This is no time to encourage violence.

This is a national crisis, and we need real leadership right now, leadership that will bring everyone to the table so we can take measures to root out systemic racism.

It's time for us to take a hard look at uncomfortable truths. It's time for us to face the deep, open wound we have in this nation.

We need justice for George Floyd.

We need real police reform that holds all cops up to the high standards that so many of them actually meet — that holds bad cops accountable, and that repairs the relationship between law enforcement and the community they are sworn to protect.

And we need to stand up as a nation — with the black community, and with all minority communities — and come together as one America. That's the challenge we face.

And it will require those of us who sit in positions of influence to finally deal with the abuse of power.

The pain is too immense for one community to bear alone. It is the duty of every American to grapple with it — and grapple with it now.

With our complacency, our silence — we are complicit in perpetuating these cycles of violence.

Nothing about this will be easy or comfortable. But if we simply allow this wound to scab over once more, without treating the underlying injury — we will never truly heal.

The very soul of America is at stake.

We must commit, as a nation, to pursue justice with every ounce of our being. We have to pursue it with real urgency. We have to make real the American promise, which we have never fully grasped: That all men and women are not only equal at creation, but throughout their lives.

Tens if not hundreds of millions of Americans agreed with this statement, line for line. Biden's remarks perfectly encapsulated the modern racial politics projected by the Democratic establishment: that Black people are being routinely and systematically hunted down and murdered by racist Whites, just as they have been for 400 years.

With these remarks, Joe Biden was messaging to America that the **institutional racism** of centuries past was alive and well, and that action must swiftly be taken to address it.

And so, America's police departments faced a wave of pressure to change how they operated, particularly in Democrat-controlled cities with significant Black populations. Throughout 2020, there were many public calls for sheriff's offices and police departments to change their approach — and in particular, to be more reserved in their use-of-force doctrines. Here, the response was marketed as one that would address the **institutional racism** that poisoned and percolated throughout the nation's law enforcement agencies.

Simultaneously, corporate America responded with pledges to increase diversity, equity, and inclusion within their ranks. Many companies committed to hiring more Blacks and other minorities in executive roles and increasing their overall workforce diversity. Bank of America, for instance, pledged $1 billion in support of racial equality just days after Floyd's death.[10] JPMorgan Chase followed suit with a $30 billion commitment for "racial equity."[11] Here, the response was marketed as one that would address **institutional racism** in banking and finance.

Additionally, there was a notable push to support Black-owned businesses through investment and partnership opportunities, aiming to close the Black-White economic gap. Uber Eats and Doordash, as notable examples, allowed users to specifically patronize Black-owned establishments. Here, the response was marketed as one that would address **institutional racism** in business.

Black scholarships, internships, and fellowships proliferated. The fairness and legitimacy of standardized tests was called into question. Educational institutions were pressured to reexamine their admission policies and programs to enhance access for underrepresented communities (Blacks) in an attempt to increase minority (Black) participation in elite educational settings. These actions represented a broad, concerted effort to leverage the momentum of the civic discord sparked by Floyd's death to create thoroughgoing changes to academic structures. Here, the response was marketed as one that would address **institutional racism** in education and professional development.

Spearheaded by America's coastal elites, social media became a reservoir for pro-Floyd hagiography. The black square movement on Instagram was the most memorable such example, but a countless variety of pastel-shaded infographics also dominated social media feeds throughout the summer of 2020. Here, the response was marketed as one that would raise awareness of **institutional racism** in society writ large.

What's the throughline here? What's the commonality between all of the responses to George Floyd's death, by Hollywood, corporate America, and various branches of government??

The focus on **INSTITUTIONAL RACISM.**

The response by all of the aforementioned groups was to address the **INSTITUTIONAL** factors ostensibly responsible for Floyd's death, and for all of the Black deaths that might plausibly be categorized alongside it.

A recap, which is reductive but not wrong:

George Floyd died ——-> millions of people demonstrated to achieve "Justice for George Floyd" ——-> the most powerful people in the world swore oaths to address America's **institutional racism**

And that has been the story for the past four years… The fires were extinguished, but the passion drummed up in 2020 was not contained within 2020…

I remember, in vivid detail, walking around downtown Dallas the day that Derek Chauvin's verdict was announced, the year after Floyd's death. I remember seeing businesses locking their doors and boarding up their windows with plywood in anticipation of an acquittal. This happened in every major city throughout the country. Amongst the demographic of urban landowners, people were terrified of a ruling that would contravene the ethos of BLM and the narrative surrounding Floyd's death. People were terrified that their cities would be destroyed as a sort of messy, nebulous act of racial retribution.

All of this is to say, the impact of Floyd's death has been definitional of the current epoch. Whether they realize it or not, the way that Americans discuss race today is tempered by how their world shifted in 2020.

That's how we got here... ... ...

Again, if you are someone who already knows all of this stuff, I am sorry to bore you. I regret that I may have wasted your time with a pedantic and meandering review of events that have been incessantly drilled into your head, for your entire life, by the nation's race-obsessed schools and media.

I lament that this segment must be a part of the book.

But I felt I had to do it. Even if you did know, I felt it necessary to prove to you that I know too...

I will not have people criticizing what I've done or what I've written on the grounds that I'm ignorant of how we've arrived at this point. I will not have people claiming that I'm unaware of the history because of my age, because of where I grew up, or because I'm not Black.

I know the history.

And I know that understanding America's record of race relations, particularly with respect to the six decades since the passage of the Civil Rights Act, is critical if the present moment is to be understood with any degree of clarity.

CHAPTER 7: THE NEED

With all of the expository legwork complete, I'll ask and answer one important question:

Why is the modern moment of American race relations best explained by this book?

The reason that the modern moment of race relations is best explained by this book is because it differentiates the phenomenon of *institutional racism* from the phenomenon of *implicit bias* in a way that even the most zealous racial narcissists should be able to understand.

And "implicit bias" isn't even the right term for what I'm talking about…

Implicit bias has become very fashionable and widely used in recent years, but the word "implicit" suggests that the holder of the views is not aware of *why* they hold them, or even *that* they hold them in the first place. For a lot of people, interpersonal racism isn't subconscious or mysterious — rather, it's a clear psychological predilection that they can feel, understand, and consciously integrate into decision making processes.

If a man is playing pickup basketball at his local YMCA, for example, and he's forced to choose between a Black guy and a White guy as potential teammates, he may feel an impulse to choose one over the other for a fundamentally racial reason. And probably, this impulse is totally intelligible to him, even when his two options are the same height, the same build, and similarly dressed. Why he leans toward choosing the Black guy is not a mystery: whenever he turns on his TV, he sees that virtually all of the professional basketball players are Black, despite Black people making up a relatively small proportion of the overall public. People have eyes. People notice things. There's nothing implicit about what's going on here.

Obviously there are an infinite number of more sinister examples I could have used… And in many of these cases, people's prejudices are totally predictable and explicable.

And so, it seems best to juxtapose the term "institutional racism" with the term "interpersonal racism" rather than the term "implicit bias."

Institutional racism and interpersonal racism are related but distinct concepts that have both historically contributed to inequalities, especially in the context of anti-Black racism in the United States.

The terms recur frequently throughout the remainder of the book, so I want to clearly convey what I think they mean.

Institutional racism refers to policies, laws, and procedures embedded within institutions that result in differential treatment based on race. If a specific college or university has a policy against admitting Blacks, as was indeed the case for many post-secondary institutions throughout American history, that college or university is engaging in institutional racism. In this case, the institution itself (and not merely the people affiliated with the institution) is operating in a way that discriminates against people based on race.

Interpersonal racism, on the other hand, involves the attitudes or impulses that affect our understanding, actions, and decisions with respect to other races. Interpersonal racism is not always overtly discriminatory like institutional racism, but it may manifest in prejudiced actions nevertheless. For instance, a high school counselor who instinctively recommends that a Black student apply to bottom-tier colleges without first knowing that student's grades may be demonstrating interpersonal racism. Here, there's a totally plausible case that the counselor's preconceptions about Black aptitude (in general) are leading her to believe that the student (specifically) should go to a bottom-tier college.

Both phenomena illustrate how racism, whether embedded in systems or expressed through personal convictions, could theoretically perpetuate disparities and discrimination against Black individuals in the United States...

These concepts don't seem that complicated to me, but for some reason they are tortuously impenetrable and deranging for a large swath of the American public....

In 2024, examples of institutional racism (against Blacks) are extremely,

extremely, extremely, extremely, extremely, extremely,
extremely, extremely, extremely, extremely, extremely,
extremely, extremely, extremely, extremely, extremely,
extremely, extremely, extremely, extremely, extremely,
extremely, extremely, extremely, extremely, extremely,
extremely, extremely, extremely, extremely, extremely,
extremely, extremely, extremely, extremely, extremely,
extremely, extremely, extremely, extremely, extremely,
extremely, extremely, extremely, extremely, extremely,
extremely, extremely, extremely, extremely, extremely,
extremely, extremely, extremely, extremely, extremely,
extremely, extremely, extremely, extremely, extremely,
extremely, extremely, extremely, extremely, extremely,
extremely, extremely, extremely, extremely, extremely,
extremely, extremely, extremely, extremely, extremely,
extremely, extremely, extremely, extremely, extremely,
extremely, extremely, extremely, extremely, extremely,
extremely, extremely, extremely, extremely, extremely,
extremely, extremely, extremely, extremely, extremely,
extremely, extremely, extremely, extremely, extremely,
extremely, extremely, extremely, extremely, extremely,
extremely, extremely, extremely, extremely, extremely,
extremely, extremely, extremely, extremely, extremely,
extremely, extremely, extremely, extremely, extremely,
extremely, extremely, extremely, extremely, extremely,
extremely, extremely, extremely, extremely, extremely,
extremely, extremely, extremely, extremely, extremely,
extremely, extremely, extremely, extremely, extremely,
extremely, extremely, extremely, extremely, extremely,
extremely, extremely, extremely, extremely, extremely,
extremely, extremely, extremely, extremely, extremely,
extremely, extremely, extremely, extremely, extremely,
extremely, extremely, extremely, extremely, extremely,
extremely, extremely, extremely, extremely, extremely,
extremely, extremely, extremely, extremely, extremely,
extremely, extremely, extremely, extremely, extremely,
extremely, extremely, extremely, extremely, extremely,
extremely, extremely, extremely, extremely, extremely,
extremely, extremely, extremely, extremely, extremely,
extremely, extremely, extremely, extremely, extremely,

extremely, extremely, extremely, extremely, extremely,
extremely, extremely, extremely, extremely, extremely,
extremely, extremely, extremely, extremely, extremely,
extremely, extremely, extremely, extremely, extremely,
extremely, extremely, extremely, extremely, extremely,
extremely, extremely, extremely, extremely, extremely,
extremely, extremely, extremely, extremely, extremely,
extremely, extremely, extremely, extremely, extremely,
extremely, extremely, extremely, extremely, extremely,
extremely, extremely, extremely, extremely, extremely,
extremely, extremely, extremely, extremely, extremely,
extremely, extremely, extremely, extremely, extremely,
extremely, extremely, extremely, extremely, extremely,
extremely, extremely, extremely, extremely, extremely,
extremely, extremely, extremely, extremely, extremely,
extremely, extremely, difficult to identify, and outward
demonstrations of interpersonal racism are also a vanishing
phenomenon.

Consider the two examples I just provided.

Universities are not allowed to discriminate against (Black)
students. And moreover, any high school counselor who is
caught doing something even conceivably racist against
(Black) students is promptly fired. It simply isn't tolerated within
the current American system. As a cultural matter, it's totally
proscribed.

Now, some people feel inclined to argue that, given the
demographic and socioeconomic realities of American society,
interpersonal racism inevitably manifests in institutional
racism. Institutions, after all, are composed of individuals.
They are composed of specific agents and decision-makers,
people who exert their wills in order to shape the world. A
White hiring manager who doesn't like Black people could, in
theory, decide not to hire any of the Black applicants who he
interviews. But again, unless the hiring manager himself has
no boss or wider corporate obligations, this is not something

that he can sustain. Regardless of what state he lives in, he will be reprimanded or fired as soon as he is found out.

The modern moment of race relations could not be understood by a book like Sprigle's, Griffin's, or Halsell's for a very simple reason: the institutional racism that they documented has vanished, and so too has much of the petty, interpersonal racism that they were subjected to.

No... Books produced in the same format as Sprigle's, Griffin's, or Halsell's wouldn't be interesting today. In all three of these cases, the authors went undercover in order to document the daily experiences of Blacks. They became Black and immersed themselves in the Black world, which was, in all of their respective eras, categorically different from the White world. The buses were different. The trains were different. The restaurants were different. The jobs were different. The schools were different. The way that Blacks were treated by courts and government agencies was different. Everything was dramatically different, and shining light on the difference was a useful journalistic endeavor.

In the '40s, in the '50s, and in the '60s, Black America and White America were segregated in a way that prevented Whites (even poor Whites) from understanding the Black experience. Blacks led lives that were qualitatively different from the lives of economically similar Whites, and this difference was significant — and therefore books about the daily experiences of a regular Black person going about their normal life seemed intensely fascinating to a vast contingent of White America.

Those days are behind us... ... ...

I've lived in Black neighborhoods. I've worked in a Black workplace. I know that documenting their lives the way that Sprigle, Griffin, and Halsell did simply wouldn't be that interesting to the average American reader.

As I outlined in the preceding chapters the civic activism and legislative developments of the past 60 years have seen the elimination of the institutional pillars that upheld the segregation and anti-Black racism of decades past. For at least four generations, a constellation of powerful, well-funded NGOs and government agencies has existed in this country with the sole purpose of seeking out and combating institutional racism wherever it has been found to exist. This mission has been pursued doggedly — to the point where no serious person would ever say that significant or meaningful forms of (anti-Black) institutional racism persist in America.

And yet, it's obvious that Blacks and Whites have a different experience in America...

Even in a country devoid of institutional racism, and even in a country where conspicuous opportunities to actualize personal bias are disappearing, there are still situations where interpersonal racism can be actualized inconspicuously.

In order to understand the Black experience in America, and American race relations more broadly, it's necessary to understand that Blacks and Whites are not treated equally in situations where they are not forced by institutions or mechanisms of social oversight to be treated equally. In some situations, Americans are free to exercise personal discretion and extend or withhold goodwill based on nothing other than their own personal disposition — based on nothing other than their own personal biases.

Hitchhiking is the best example I can think of.

When a driver approaches someone who is standing on the side of the road with their arm extended and thumb upright, a very clear social dynamic exists:

The driver is free, if he or she so chooses, to pull over...

But there is no social consequence for not pulling over. The driver can pretend they don't see the hitchhiker, and no ramifications will follow... Nobody will scoff at them or glare at them... Nobody will chastise them on social media, write them up to HR, or file a police report against them for committing a hate crime...

If the hitchhiker seems threatening, unseemly, or off-putting in any way, the driver can just keep driving. And then, in an instant, the hitchhiker becomes a blip in the rearview mirror. In an instant, the hitchhiker disappears from the driver's world, and so too does the decision not to pull over.

Hitchhiking presents a unique social dynamic. It is an interaction where traditional norms and expectations of non-discrimination are suspended, giving way to the primacy of personal discretion. In this scenario, the driver possesses unilateral authority to make a snap judgment about whether to offer a ride to a stranger based on whatever criteria they deem relevant.

This decision-making process is not subject to social scrutiny or ethical condemnation, largely because there is no societal expectation or obligation for the driver to pick up any hitchhiker at all. As such, the driver is free to employ their own set of criteria — including factors such as age, dress, sex, and yes, **race** — in making their choice.

When you are on the shoulder of a road, people are allowed to discriminate against you.

This freedom essentially allows for what might be termed *socially sanctioned discrimination* or **shoulder racism**. The private nature of an individual's vehicle as a personal space that is not open to the public supports the notion that the driver has the right to control entry. As a society, we accept that the safety concerns inherent in inviting unknown individuals into a personal vehicle justify this discretionary practice. Thus, while in most public or semi-public settings, such discriminatory preferences would be deemed unacceptable or even illegal, in the context of hitchhiking, they are the standard. This scenario encapsulates a complex interplay between notions of personal safety, private property rights, and social norms around discrimination — and it's one that is tremendously useful for understanding expressions of racism.

Hitchhiking exposes real sentiments that might otherwise be concealed. It reveals what is truly in the hearts and minds of the American people. It reveals how they act when nobody is telling them how to act.

And so, I decided to make *Seven Shoulders* a book about hitchhiking.

More specifically, it's a book about soliciting rides while standing on the side of the road.

At no point in the process of writing this book did I actually get into the strangers' cars or accept rides to the places that I claimed I was heading.

Rather, I set out to see how difficult it would be to solicit a ride while standing at seven different shoulders throughout the country, first as a White man, and then again as a Black man on the following day. In each place I visited, I arrived at the shoulder of a highway, faced the oncoming traffic, stuck my thumb up, and then waited until someone pulled over to offer me a ride. Whenever someone pulled over, I would pretend to be traveling to a location that is in a different direction than the one that they were headed so that I would have an excuse to not get in the vehicle.

If nobody stopped to offer a ride after two hours, I would retire for the day.

Unlike Sprigle and Griffin, I did not confine my experiment to the South. Unlike them, I was not looking to document and expose the institutional racism of this specific region. As I said, I don't think that would have yielded a particularly interesting book. Times have changed. In the modern era, there is no anthropological account I could give of Southern institutions that would captivate the nation in the way that my predecessors did.

Rather, this book seeks to expose the surviving form of racism — the interpersonal racism that manifests in the individual judgements of regular people, virtually all of whom would recoil at allegations of racial bigotry. And the thing about this interpersonal racism is that it isn't endemic to the South. Interpersonal racism is a feature of all Americans. Accordingly, I visited numerous areas across the country.

There is no particular rhyme or reason that explains why I chose the seven different places I went to, but I do feel like I exposed myself to a sufficiently varied sample of America to draw the conclusions that I draw.

I took statistics courses in university. I took social science research methodology courses. I've been lectured about sample collection and regression analysis and hypothesis testing. I understand that this isn't perfect…   … but I do think it's good.

Sooooooo….

That's my explanation. That's why this book is the way it is. That's why I went to the shoulders.

To understand racism in the modern era is to understand how people are treated in situations where they are subjected to genuine discretion ….

In situations where they are *on the shoulder*…

… when charity or cold indifference can be shown to them without the attendance of any broader social consequences…

PART TWO: SHOULDERS ON THE ROAD

CHAPTER 8: BECOMING BLACK

In order to pose as a Black hitchhiker, I first needed to figure out how to become Black…

… which is actually more challenging than one might expect.

There isn't a lot of useful advice out there. You can't just Google it. If you search "Wikihow blackface", for example, the top result is a wikiHow article titled "How to Tell if You Are a Racist: 13 Steps (with Pictures)".

I didn't have time to read the article. I'm sure I would have been beyond salvage in the author's mind…   Whatever…

A whole bunch of other articles also popped up, mostly with titles along the lines of "Why you should never do blackface," and "Here's why blackface is racist."

……………….. Righhtttttttttttttttttttttttttttttttttttt   …………………..

Anyway, there isn't a lot of guidance online, and asking a real human in real life was totally out of the question, for obvious reasons.

Naturally, I considered how my predecessors went about their transformations.

Sprigle's transformation was relatively basic. After experimenting with a range of lotions, liquids, and unguents, and after consulting with numerous chemists about the application of phenol compounds, all to no avail, Sprigle decided to try creating an infusion from mahogany bark.

Convinced that this would be the winning solution, he ordered a hundred-pound bale of the material from Nicaragua.

When the mahogany bark proved unsuccessful in producing the desired change in skin tone, he simply decided to burn himself in the sun. Three weeks of intensive tanning in Florida gave him a "passable coffee-with-plenty-of-cream shade."

Sprigle's transformation was completed with black-rimmed glasses and a cap that "drooped like a tam-o'-shanter" to cover his bald head. I guess this worked out for him just fine. As Sprigle mentions, passing as Black in the 1940s was largely a question of how someone presented and positioned themself in public. If a man who had coffee-with-plenty-of-cream-colored skin sat in the Black section of trains, patronized Black cafes, and traveled with an exclusively Black entourage, nobody would suspect that he was anything other than Black.

Griffin's transformation was more... ... ... *ballsy*... .... It was more radical.

After arriving in New Orleans, Griffin immediately contacted numerous dermatologists to discuss possible darkening measures. One of these doctors agreed to meet with him and promptly prescribed oral doses of methoxsalen, an anti-vitiligo drug. In combination with extended exposure to UV rays from a sunlamp, the methoxsalen caused Griffin to become dark-skinned within a week. The customary timeline for methoxsalen treatment was anywhere from six to twelve weeks, but because Griffin could not afford to wait that long, he significantly upped his dosage...

And he paid a price for it... Griffin complains throughout the book of feeling constantly on the verge of throwing up, and he was even forced to do blood tests to ensure that the abuse he was subjecting his liver to would not become fatal.

Lacking Afro-textured hair, Griffin shaved his head. Any remaining patches of light skin that managed to evade the UV rays or drug treatment were blotted out with a dark stain.

All of the pictures I've seen of Griffin as a Black man are quite convincing. They're sort of grainy, as one would expect, but he did seem to look totally and undeniably Black. The pain seems to have been worth it.

Halsell met with Griffin prior to undertaking her experiment, and so the similarities between her transition and his are not all that surprising.

Like Griffin, Halsell consulted numerous medical doctors in advance of her darkening. And like Griffin, she was convinced that the optimal course of action was to take oral doses of the anti-vitiligo medication in concert with prolonged exposure to UV radiation.

In preparation for her first portion of the book, the Harlem stint, she suntanned on the beaches of Puerto Rico, taking her pills before each session so that the photosensitizing drug could accelerate the darkening of her skin's pigmentation.

Throughout her time in New York, she lost a bit of her color, which prompted a migration to the U.S. Virgin Islands to regain her desired hue before beginning the second phase of her Black life in the American South.

Halsell had blue eyes, like me, so she took advantage of the new contact lens technology in order to achieve a racially coherent, brown-eyed look. Had she been born a few decades earlier, it's possible that she wouldn't have been able to pass as Black regardless of how dark her skin became.

I didn't get especially creative with my transformation. I didn't go overboard. I didn't feel I needed to. Then again, I also didn't feel like I could.

It wasn't as if there was anyone who I could ask for help. I couldn't go to a dermatologist. I couldn't present a medical doctor with the request of turning me into a Black man. And nor could I even consult a makeup or costume professional. It's a different era. There was nobody I could turn to for help. Unlike the journalists who had gone before me, I had to figure out my transformation alone.

I was pragmatic. I came up with something that worked.

I don't know how developed the beauty and cosmetics industry was in the Jim Crow era, but I am a bit surprised that some sort of makeup-oriented transformation wasn't the obvious first choice for my predecessors. I guess they were probably less worried about skin cancer and the health effects of turbo-dosing relatively new and obscure pharmaceuticals.

In any case, I was convinced that a regular, commercially available, brown-colored foundation would be sufficient for me to achieve the necessary skin tone. The particular one I landed on was Maybelline's "Mocha" shade — slightly darker than their "Coconut" product, but not quite as dark as "Java." I figured it was best not to get too ambitious.

I didn't really feel like shaving my head, so I opted to go for an Afro wig, which would also serve the purpose of signaling my race more clearly to approaching cars while I stood on the shoulders.

My eyebrows could be darkened with a tinted pomade — a product that apparently comes in a thousand varieties.

To deal with the issue of eye color, I simply picked out a pair of brown contact lenses.

Buying the wig and the contact lenses was not that strange of an experience. I got these items at a costume store in Montreal before leaving for the States. I wasn't paranoid during the purchase. I think the checkout lady probably just thought I was trying to pull off some sort of swarthy pirate look.

And more probably, the checkout lady didn't even give my purchase a second thought. It's true that I bought these items from a costume store, but it may as well have been a sex shop. The people in Montreal are such sickos that most of the other clients were clearly just picking out twisted new kinkfuel — lots of animal masks and handcuffs and steampunk paraphernalia and stuff like that. I'm sure the checkout lady

74

there deals with so many freaks and debauchees that my Afro and contact lenses didn't even raise her suspicions.

Buying the foundation and the tinted eyebrow pomade was more nerve-racking. I got this stuff from a CVS across the street from Vanderbilt's Central Library. A Black girl was working the till, and I felt the urge to tell her that I was buying the products for my girlfriend, which seems kind of funny in hindsight. I'm sure that was already her assumption. I'm sure her assumption was not, "Hey, I bet this guy is buying these Afro-oriented cosmetic products so that he can produce a modern adaptation of John Howard Griffin's *Black Like Me*."

In hindsight, a lot of paranoia I felt throughout the trip lacked justification. Nobody suspected what I was doing.

One factor that made the transformation less stressful and strenuous is the fact that I really didn't need to show much skin. Despite the fact that I would be traveling in the summer heat, I figured it would be easiest to wear pants and long-sleeve shirts so that I would have a minimal area of exposure. I wore black jeans and dark gray shirts to reduce the risk of noticeable makeup smears.

All things considered, I did a good job. I wasn't a movie-grade transracialist by any stretch. If footage of the Black me was shown on an IMAX screen, I'm sure someone in the theater would eventually spot a cream-colored blemish or an errant brown hair.

But I didn't need to be that good. I just needed to blend in. I just needed to get by. Ultimately, I just needed to convince the drivers who approached my spot on the shoulder that I was, in fact, Black.

CHAPTER 9: DOES THIS COUNT?

Is what I am doing actually blackface?

It's an interesting question… I've thought a great deal about whether or not to embrace the term.

I do think the term *journalistic blackface* is good, though I feel compelled to make a few comments about it.

As I mentioned in the book's introduction, blackface has traditionally been understood as a visual phenomenon. It is a visual act, and the performative component that has always been an essential feature of blackface is premised on the ability of others to observe the *visual* image of the blackfaced person.

And importantly, this performative component is also premised on the ability of others to **recognize** what they are observing. As I've always understood traditional forms of blackface, it's essential for people to know what they are looking at.

In that sense, I am not *really* doing blackface. Nobody who sees me knows that I am actually a White man. They think that I am Black. And so, I am not really putting on a performance in the way that blackfaced individuals normally do. I am not walking out into the street as a White man, applying the makeup in plain view of the public, and then jumping up and down while acting like a cartoonish minstrel caricature.

Like I said, I'm not even publishing the pictures. I'm simply becoming Black because I am a visionary writer who wants to demystify race in a way that is creative, compelling, and beautiful. I'm not making a big scene about it. I'm simply doing it while going about my business.

If one uses a deep, culturally curious definition of blackface, what I'm doing doesn't count…

A strict dictionary definition, however, suggests that it probably does count:

black·face| ˈblak͵fās |

noun

> 1 used to refer to the practice of wearing makeup to imitate the appearance of a black person. The use of such makeup was associated with minstrel shows in the United States from the 1830s until the mid 20th century; it is now regarded as highly offensive: *he appeared in blackface | [as modifier] : blackface minstrels.*

I am wearing makeup to imitate the appearance of a Black person. That is very much the case. And so, according to the New Oxford American Dictionary, I am doing blackface.

Hmmmm….

Journalistic blackface seems fine. I can't think of a better term. If you've read this far, it should be clear to you what I am doing.

CHAPTER 10: NOTES ON HITCHHIKING

I've hitchhiked a few times before in real life. Choosing a good spot is arguably the most important part of the process. I have no reason to believe that the basic selection strategies I use would be any less sensible for a Black man than they are for a White man.

Here are some guidelines I try to abide by:

1. **Visibility**: Ensure that the shoulder you choose offers high visibility and provides drivers ample time to see you. A long, straight stretch of road before the spot can be prime as it allows drivers to clock you from a distance and then decide whether or not to stop.

2. **Stopping Opportunity**: Look for a location where drivers can easily and safely pull over without disrupting traffic. Wide shoulders, rest areas, or parking lots just off the main road tend to be solid choices. Don't waste time in areas where stopping might be dangerous or illegal, such as bends, narrow shoulders, or no-stopping zones.

3. **Traffic Speed**: Areas where vehicles are moving at slower speeds are preferable, as drivers are more likely to stop. Entry points to interstates and major thoroughfares are strategic because the merging vehicles have more time to notice you and react.

4. **Driver Mentality**: Choose spots where drivers are likely to be more amenable to picking up hitchhikers. Finding shoulders near stations, rest areas, or just after leaving a town can be effective because drivers are more relaxed and can take a moment to assess you as a potential passenger.

5. **Safety and Legality**: Try to consider the safety and legality of your pickup spot. Some areas have explicit laws regarding hitchhiking in certain parts of the roadway system, especially on ramps and interstates. If you're going to contravene a state's hitchhiking laws, or if you can't even determine what the state's laws actually are, try your best to be inconspicuous. Don't hug the road too closely. Stand a few paces back so that you can hit the ditch if need be.

6. **Proximity to Urban Centers**: While being close to urban areas can increase your chances due to higher traffic volumes, it's also more likely that local, short-distance traffic won't be headed toward your endpoint, and therefore won't be willing to stop. Don't be too close to downtown. Weigh the benefit of potentially more rides against the likelihood of finding a driver going a further distance.

Having Google Street View is a huge asset when trying to find the ideal shoulder. I scoped out all of my spots in advance, and all of them met my basic expectations, if not always being as spacious as I would have preferred. Most of the shoulders I ended up at were on the outskirts of the cities, alongside interstate on-ramps or merging lanes.

As far as I can tell, the hitchhiking community is divided on the question of whether or not it's useful to hold a sign indicating your destination. On the one hand, it can obviously help weed out people who will soon be turning off in a totally different direction. On the other hand, there are some drivers who will instinctively refuse to pull over for someone whose terminus is beyond their own, failing to reach the obvious conclusion that most hitchhikers are willing to travel in multiple stages. I didn't have a sign because, again, I wasn't actually trying to go anywhere. I was just trying to get people to stop. Whenever someone would pull over, I would simply invent a destination that I knew wouldn't be compatible with their own travel plans.

I offer up all of this added context because I feel it helps to clarify the format of my experiment — and also the decision-making process behind that format.

I trust that for most readers, the act of transracial hitchhiking isn't an especially familiar topic.

CHAPTER 11: NASHVILLE

Nashville in White

My flight from LaGuardia arrives late in the afternoon. It's hot down here — probably 90 degrees. I'm tired of summer. I have had too much of it lately. Owing to various journalistic stints in South America, I skipped North America's most recent winter. I'm looking forward to writing the book, but not to idling outside under the sun. I burn easily and am unusually prone to bouts of heat stroke. Sometimes they are debilitating. In this sense, I am the furthest thing from a Black man. I suppose that's part of the reason why I opted for makeup rather than the beach or tanning bed.

I line up to get on the shuttle bus toward downtown. I do not have cash, but a dopey-looking man who is roughly my age offers to cover my fare so that I don't have to hunt down an ATM. He is an affable character, and we riff on the ride. We take the shuttle bus through the eastern part of the city towards Music Row, where my hotel is.

Downtown is moving. People are already starting to fill the karaoke bars. For years, social media has given me the impression that every woman who has her bachelorette party outside of Vegas has it in Nashville. The countless Millennials I come across who are covered from head to toe in bedazzled cowgirl regalia affirm this.

After checking in to my hotel and dropping off my bag, I head toward the first shoulder, which I surveyed on Street View in advance. It's a few miles from the hotel, and I've been compressed in Spirit's economy class all afternoon, so I decide to walk.

Nashville is one of the nicer cities in America. Aside from the relative cleanliness, order, and attainable prosperity that distinguish it from the nation's other urban centers, there is a qualitative force that contributes to the texture of life.

There is a rhythm, a vibration, a pulse... or something of the sort that crawls into your body through every available hole. There's the smell of barbecue, heavy, inviting. People smile. They welcome. They understand. They are loud and boorish, but it's folksy. It's endearing. The city itself is a song, a subtle, complex tune. It's a place of stories, of life written in music notes, clichéd and twangy though they may be. The meat is smoked. The smiles warm. This is what occupies my mind as I walk across Centennial Park toward the western edge of the city.

Technically speaking, I am about to commit a crime... At least, that is my understanding of Tennessee state law 558-139: "No person shall stand in a roadway for the purpose of soliciting a ride or employment from the occupant of any vehicle." Violation is a Class C misdemeanor. And yet, here I am musing about the city's whimsical charm rather than worrying about being arrested.

Is this a sign of White privilege? I don't know how to answer something like that.

Boyish whimsy is its own form of privilege, of course, but nobody gets mad about that.

The spot itself is fine. It's a fine shoulder. I was expecting a bit more space. I was expecting the shoulder to be slightly wider. Because I am at a fork between an on-ramp and a service road, cars are passing me on both sides, which is less than ideal. From the Street View images, it didn't seem like the service road would be so close behind me.

But it will do. I dig my feet into the thin layer of gravel the same way a batter would before squaring up to home plate. The count is 0-0. I start the timer on my phone. Then I throw my arm out, and my thumb pops up.

It's been a while since I've done this. And it's been even longer since I've done it sober. It's a weird feeling… to just be standing in the middle of the road… brazenly begging strangers to let you in their car. It feels a little bit like what I imagine it would feel like to show up to a department store completely naked, unabashedly looking for a set of clothes.

Ummmm… yes, hello…. I would like to…. buy some clothes please…

"BUT SIR, WHY AREN'T YOU ALREADY WEARING CLOTHES??" Such a question would surely be asked by the store's employees with the same urgency as "BUT SIR, WHY AREN'T YOU ALREADY IN A CAR??" is undoubtedly being asked by the drivers passing me by.

Why is your cock out? Why are you not in a car? These are basically the same question.

They don't get it. They don't understand me. I feel like nobody understands me. They want me to get a grip. Everybody wants me to get a grip.

47 minutes pass by. Then something good happens. A guy in a Chevy pickup truck, clearly a working man, clearly driving a company vehicle, pulls to the side of the road 30 feet behind me. I pivot and approach the window.

"Where are you headed?" He seems safe enough. I would get in if I actually were trying to catch a ride.

"I'm trying to get to Little Rock," I lie. Little Rock is sufficiently far away, I figure, that the chances he is on his way there are very small.

"I can take you to Dickson; it's 'round 30 miles west of here," he tells me.

"Ahh…" I sigh, rubbing the back of my neck. "I'm sorta' looking for a straight shot."

He looks confused. "You're going to have a tough time getting there in one go," he advises.

I thank him anyway. Before he pulls away, I tell him that I've been out here for a while, and I ask why he stopped.

"Why not? You seemed like a clean-enough guy."

Clean enough? I'm standing here with my proverbial cock out, and you think I'm a "clean-enough guy"?

Whatever…

I'll take it.

Nashville in Black

I didn't get much sleep.

I was nervous, and I am nervous now… which is natural, I suppose…. I've never done this before. That probably goes without saying, but I'll say it anyway.

I have been White — glaringly and unabashedly — since the day I was born.

After shaving and showering, I'm ready to undergo the full transformation for the first time.

I surveil myself in the bathroom mirror for a moment before opening the small cardboard box that contains the brown contact lenses. I opt to get the colored contacts in before my hands are caked in makeup. That seems like the prudent thing to do.

I've never worn contacts before, so getting them in seems like it will be the most challenging part of the transformation. I assume that they're ready to wear right out of the package, but I rinse them in the cleaning solution just to be sure.

I watched a few YouTube tutorials in preparation. I read the instructional manual multiple times. The conventional wisdom, I learned, is that you're supposed to use your non-dominant hand to restrain your upper eyelid while using the middle finger of your dominant hand to restrain your lower eyelid, which leaves your dominant index finger free to plop the lens directly on your cornea.

I try this for close to an hour. Little teardrops slide down my cheek. *It's purely autonomic, purely somatic… It's not because I'm a pussy.* That's what I tell myself.

Over the course of the past 26 years, I've developed a very practical aversion to having objects come directly into contact with my eyes. Every time I try the recommended application method, I flinch very hard at the last moment, causing the lens to either shake free from my finger before even touching my eye, or causing the lens to fall on my eye so unevenly that it bounces off into the sink.

Maybe this is God's way of telling me to write a book about something else.

No… That can't be it…

After a great deal of trial and error, I find that I can slowly introduce objects to the inside of my bottom eyelid without flinching as much. If I leave my upper eyelid alone, I can stretch out the lower eyelid to create a sort of fleshy pocket to rest the lens in. Once it's securely resting in that little pocket, I violently jerk my head back, in much the same way a cormorant will jerk his head back to manage an oversized carp down his elastic gullet.

Finally, after many failed attempts, the cormorant method works. As my head tilts, the lens falls into place. It's in. For a brief moment, everything turns brown. I blink a few times to center things. The world becomes clear, though noticeably less clear than a few moments before.

The second eye also takes multiple attempts, but it goes in much quicker than the first.

Then I dump the contents of the CVS bag onto the counter.

I grab the eyebrow pomade pen, swirl it around on the coin-sized container that holds the greasy black substance, and then apply a coat to each brow. The mirror's image becomes increasingly strange.

Next, the foundation. I apply big dollops all over my face, neck, and collar bone. I grab the foam egg I purchased to help with the application, and then I start to blend it in.

This takes longer than I expected. Patches of pale seem to refuse my advances.

But I even things out. I get into the nooks and crevices around my eyes, ears, and nose. Because I am wearing a long-sleeve shirt and pants, the proportion of my skin that I need to color is relatively small.

My teeth suddenly look so white. *They couldn't have been so white this whole time… There's no way…*

I put the Afro on, and I tuck away a lock of brown hair. I use the camera on my phone to see how things look from the back... Believably Black, I think.

Elevator. Lobby. Outside. All of it in one uninterrupted descent.

Yes, hello, world. It's me.

It's very warm. The sun lights up my brown cheeks. People pass by.

As I expected, my ambient level of paranoia is higher than usual, but the lack of foot traffic in Nashville means that I come face-to-face with relatively few people as I walk back to the shoulder. Apart from Music Row, pedestrianism is not really a thing in this city. It seems like every building I walk past has a valet lane manned by young men in collared shirts — even casual restaurants and three-star hotels. Like most of the country, the people here are largely allergic to walking… This is one of the reasons why everyone is so fat, and it's one of the reasons I love Montreal. I miss Montreal already.

The people I do encounter on the walk, with few exceptions, are White, which is a relief. I am not at all worried about White people seeing through my disguise. I do genuinely believe that my transformation is good enough for me to move through the world without raising any suspicions, **but even if it weren't**, the chances that a White person would question me are infinitesimally small……… **for obvious reasons**.

If you fraudulently present yourself as Black to a White person, they have to be 100% certain that you aren't in order to call you out. That's one of the most well-understood rules of being White. And actually, they have to be more than 100%. A mere 100% is not enough.

I arrive back at the forked shoulder between the on-ramp and the service road. Again, it's hot and late in the day. I wish there were a few trees around to keep the sun off me. *Can I burn even while I'm wearing the foundation? Is this stuff sunproof?* Hmmm…

In any case, my skin feels hotter.

I plant my feet and start the timer.

The cars pass me by to get on the interstate. Most of the drivers are White or Latino. Some of them are Black. I look further down the road at the oncoming traffic than I did yesterday. I do this because I am more paranoid about cops than I was yesterday.

I don't know what I would tell a cop if he arrested me or asked to see my driver's license. I have not invested much time in preparing for these eminently plausible contingencies.

What would I even say? *"It's not what it looks like!"?*

I don't even know what it looks like.

I see a couple of the same cars that passed me by yesterday. They don't seem to notice me.

For the first hour and a half, nobody pulls over.

At the 91-minute mark, two older guys in a silver SUV slow to a stop just behind me. One is White and one is Latino. The White guy is in his mid-fifties. The Latino could be anywhere in age from 30 to 65. Funny how that works.

I brush the twists of hair from my face and approach the passenger-side window, now rolled down.

"What's your destination?" asks the White driver from across the cab of the vehicle. It seems like such a formal register given the context, as if he were a train conductor validating my first-class fare.

"Little Rock," I lie. I try to speak normally, but I know that my voice drops an octave to meet my internalized expectations of what my voice would sound like if I really were Black.

"No sir, we ain't goin' that far," he says, "But we can take you a few miles further down the interstate before we turn off." Both men are smiling more than I am comfortable with.

"I appreciate that, but I'm looking for a straight shot."

The two men interrupt their smirks to share a confused look.

"Hey, by the way, what made you pull over? I've been out here for a while, and nobody has stopped."

"I've never had a bad time with hitchhikers," the driver tells me, which is met by a chuckle from the Latino. "As a matter of fact, I've only ever had good times."

I nod, and smile, and thank them... ... ...   and then pace backwards as they pull away.

I... think they were gay... ... ... I...   I think the driver wanted to fuck me.

CHAPTER 12: ATLANTA

Atlanta in White

I arrive late in the afternoon. I go straight downtown.

This city is massive and sprawling, but not very grandiose. It's sort of like if someone copied and pasted Albany or Rochester next to itself a dozen times.

Some people call it a *Black Mecca* — a point of congregation for blacks who are optimistic and upwardly mobile.

Sounds a bit dramatic to me, but I suppose it's as true of Atlanta as it is of any city.

I wonder if I'd want to move to Atlanta if I were Black. *Would the density and prominence of Black culture play a major role in how I decided which cities and states to spend time in? Would I still have a soft spot for places like Wyoming or Colorado if I really were Black?*

Hmmmmmm…

I quickly check in to my hotel, and then I head back out onto the street. I am in the Five Points district, just a couple blocks south of the downtown core. It's messy. I encounter the usual squalor that entrenches itself in these sorts of places.

I see a vagrant. He sits against a hot brick wall. His world is a crumbling cardboard bed. His clothes are tattered. His beard is a wild, tangled forest. His eyes are vacant plots. They've seen much — I can confidently say — too much.

I keep my pace. His eyes lift. They meet mine — a mistake on my part. The city's hum rumbles on. The moment stretches. The world shrinks. His threadbare existence quails casually against the city's towering might. This place is not his Mecca; he is not on a pilgrimage.

"A dolla' fo' some food? Jussneedadolla', missuh."

I see the empty bottles scattered around him. I shake my head, regretfully but sternly.

I keep walking.

In the few hundred yards between my hotel and the train station, I am solicited for cash by three other men whose descriptions approximate that of the first man.

It's bad out here.

I go underground to get on the MARTA train that will take me to the shoulder of the road.

The train is muggy. It's almost 90 degrees outside. If the car I'm riding in has air-conditioning, it doesn't seem to be working. I run my hand through my hair and feel glad that I am not wearing the Afro today.

I get out at the end of the line and walk half a mile to the spot that I have previously scouted out on Google Maps.

I'm in a neighborhood on the west side of the city. It's a very Black area. Most of the cars that go by as I walk have Black drivers. They look at me curiously as I make my way down the side of the road.

There are quite a few people on quads and dirtbikes. A teenage boy flies past me on a blue four-stroke wearing nothing but shorts and Nike slides. It's not what I'd wear. I wouldn't want to be going as fast as he is going while wearing what he is wearing.

Black youths have a peculiar affinity for quads and dirtbikes. Anyone who has spent time in major American cities is acutely familiar with the phenomenon — the so-called "rideout" culture.

If you aren't familiar, the following paragraphs may be interesting.

It's tough to talk about rideouts in a purely descriptive way when they've robbed you of so many hours of sleep. I feel it's best that I outsource this task to an academic:

> *Dirt bike and ATV riding on city streets —*
> *"Bike Life" — has emerged as a*
> *controversial urban subculture. Ride-outs*
> *— communal groups of ATV and dirt bike*
> *riders who perform stunts and weave*
> *through traffic — have become increasingly*
> *common on city streets across the country*
> *and the globe. These ride-outs serve as*
> *cultural performances of resistance for*
> *riders, yet are a nuisance to many others.*[12]

Cultural performances of resistance…..

Hmmmmmmm…… Basically, the point is to ride as dangerously and domineeringly as possible without dying. Almost invariably, the vehicles are not street-legal. It's all very brazen, and there is, generally speaking, no real attempt by law-enforcement to confront those who are involved.

The academic elaborates:

> *As the number of riders has proliferated,*
> *many police departments have instituted*
> *"no-chase" policies. As a result, police will*
> *not chase dirt bike and ATV riders when*
> *they commit traffic violations, since such a*
> *chase would exacerbate already unsafe*
> *driving and pedestrian conditions when*
> *there is a swarm of bikers participating in a*
> *ride-out. For example, Washington DC's*

*new police policy explains: Riders of ATVs
and dirt bikes are openly breaking the law
on DC streets. These riders do all kinds of
tricks such as wheelies and riding on the
sidewalks. ATVs and dirt bikes are illegal to
ride on public streets in the District of
Columbia, but MPD's chase policy prohibits
officers from pursuing the vehicles. In fact,
those familiar with the problem say that
some riders come from other areas on
stolen dirt bikes and ATVs because DC is
known for its no chase policy.*

I offer this note because the ride-outs really are a big part of
city life these days. They make it significantly more challenging
for the average citizen to operate. That's my take as a White
person anyway…. I do wonder if my view of ride-outs would
be more favorable in a world where I really was Black.

My attention shifts back to cars as I arrive at the shoulder.
Once again, it's not as spacious a shoulder as I assumed it
would be from the Street View, but I think it will suffice.

Cars come from opposite directions before turning left and
right onto the ramp. The ones turning left have more time to
see me, but the ones turning right are already on my side of
the road. I pace back and forth every few minutes, trying to
optimize my visibility.

My thumb points up as I offer friendly glances to the passing
drivers. I receive many strange looks. Some people squint at
me.

*Boy, what'chu doin? You ain't got no sense lookin' fo' a ride
out here on side the damn road.*

I stand there, and I smile, and I solicit…

An hour and 18 minutes pass before a guy — White and likely in his late twenties — pulls his blue Honda Civic to the side of the road.

He rolls down his window. I approach.

"Are you going to Lithia Springs? I could take you that far."

"I'm trying to get to Chattanooga, actually," I say.

He looks confused… understandably.

Seeing another car approaching from behind, he starts to creep forward, but as he does, I tell him that I've been out here for a while, and I ask why he stopped.

"You look like a chill guy," he discerned, smiling and nodding.

I say thanks and tell him to take care.

Atlanta in Black

Getting the contacts in is still difficult, and it feels like I'll never get good enough to do it on the first try.

The despair reminds me of the first few hours of learning stick shift, when every movement feels painfully graceless and maladroit. I blink, and then I blink some more. I drop each lens half a dozen times. Finally the left lens stays in. And then the right one. Again, the second lens goes in much quicker than the first.

The tinted pomade coats the eyebrows. The foundation is applied, and then blended as best as I can. I look sort of like a tall, very-dark-skinned Mexican at this point. But then I tuck my hair away and the Afro goes on… and then I look completely Black. The transformation is complete. I am Black. I don't look merely swarthy or Latin at this point. I look unmistakably Black.

I stare at myself in the mirror for a minute or two, focusing on the little crevices and contours of my face. *You are Black. You are Black. You are Black.*

The bit of skin between my eyelid and brow catches my attention. *Is it too pale?* I touch it up with the blender. *Yeah, that should be fine,* I think to myself.

Of course, I don't really know what "fine" means in this context. I don't know what benchmark I'm using. What does *fine* look like? I feel nervous about going downstairs out into the world.

My phone is sitting on the bathroom counter, playing Kanye's "Through the Wire." I love it. His jaw was mangled, his mouth wired shut, and he still got in the booth.

Making art is not easy.

I ride down the elevator alone. The doors open to the lobby. This isn't Nashville. My stomach tries to jump up. Everyone is Black. The concierge glances up from his computer screen and nods at me as I walk towards the door. I nod back as I put my sunglasses on. *Does he notice me?* I am very paranoid.

I walk out onto the street and hear the ringing of a preacher through a cheap speaker system. A small crowd of idlers has gathered around him.

> *Hear me, my brothers and sisters, as we*
> *stand on these streets of Atlanta, the spirit*
> *of our ancestors moves among us, calling*
> *us to remember who we truly are. We are*
> *not merely the descendants of those*
> *brought here in chains; we are the children*
> *of Israel, the chosen ones of the Most High!*

The preacher is really belting it out. He is a big man — a man whose colossal build seems to make his voice louder, deeper, and more arresting.

*Long have we wandered in this land, far
from our home, subjected to trials and
tribulations. But do not despair, for our story
is the story of Joseph, sold into bondage
but destined for greatness. As it was said in
the Book of Deuteronomy, we have faced
the curse of scattering, yet the time of
awakening is upon us. Look around, see
the signs of the times.*

He gesticulates. He's a good speaker.

*The world is in turmoil, but it is written, and
it shall come to pass in the last days, that
the mountain of the Lord's house shall be
established in the top of the mountains, and
shall be exalted above the hills; and all
nations shall flow unto it.' We are
witnessing the days of prophecy, the days
of our rising!*

The man's flock, composed almost entirely of middle-aged
men, nods along. The occasional "amen" is put forth in
affirmation.

*My brothers, we have been downtrodden,
yes, but like the phoenix, we shall rise from
the ashes, for our strength is not just in our
flesh but in our spirit, in the enduring
promise of the Most High. Our legacy is not
one of perpetual bondage but of eventual
triumph. And my brothers, I must say,
inevitable triumph. We will triumph because
God wants us to triumph. He has spoken it
— and my brothers, hear me when I say
that we need to listen!*

I think the volume on the speaker's sound system is maxed out. I'm sure the man's voice can be heard from five blocks away in every direction.

> *My brothers, we are the true descendants*
> *of Abraham, Isaac, and Jacob. Our heritage*
> *is not merely of slavery and oppression but*
> *of kings and prophets. We must reclaim our*
> *identity, our rightful place as the people of*
> *the covenant. So let us unite, brothers and*
> *sisters, not just in our shared past of*
> *suffering but in our future of redemption.*
> *Let us turn back to the laws and*
> *commandments given to us, for in them lies*
> *our path to liberation. The world may deny*
> *us, but the truth of our lineage cannot be*
> *erased. We are not forgotten, not forsaken.*
> *Our journey has been long, but the*
> *promised land awaits. It is time to awaken,*
> *to rise, and to reclaim our destiny as the*
> *true Hebrew Israelites, God's true chosen*
> *ones!*

I have heard and witnessed many scenes like this before. I saw it fairly often when I lived in Dallas and New York. These sorts have a presence in basically every city that has a significant Black population, though it does seem particularly common in Atlanta.

As far as sources of urban noise pollution go, it's not that bad. The sermons can have a certain rhythm to them, especially if you're in a charitable, reverent mood.

I continue walking until I get to the MARTA station and take the westbound train to HE Holmes Station. The ride is uneventful. There are several old, poorly dressed men on one side of the car, but they talk amongst themselves. I stay on my side and look down at my phone.

We arrive at HE Holmes. I disembark and use an underpass to cross the interstate. It's 90 degrees again, and drizzling intermittently. I'm sweating quite a bit, but the foundation doesn't seem to streak or run. Cheers, Maybelline!

I envision myself as a brand ambassador.

"Trust me, this stuff is *life-changing*!" I tell the camera, encircled by a blinding ring light.

I get bored. I think it would be interesting to count the cars.

One, two, three, four, five… I get to 17 before giving up.

I experiment with arm position and thumb angle. Surely there's an optimal posture to seem conspicuous but not threatening or psychopathic. Sticking your arm outright at 90 degrees is too zealous. Sticking your thumb up so aggressively that it bends backward is too zealous. Your thumb shouldn't have a boner. It should be turgid, somewhat, but not rock-hard. I think the best way to do it is to give your arm some slack by bringing your elbow slightly inward, as if you are genuinely (but casually) giving the passing cars a thumbs-up, as if their entrance onto the ramp genuinely makes you proud.

Again, it's the late afternoon. It's not busy enough that southbound cars would be prevented from stopping at the yield sign, nor northbound cars from pulling over on the side of the ramp.

I readjust the wig, ever so slightly, by fixing a loose strand of hair the same way I imagine a Black person would.

One hour passes. Yesterday's hour and 18 minute mark passes. I prefer being out here than downtown because the people are far enough away to alleviate the paranoia of being exposed.

One hour and 45 minutes. No luck.

Everyone who gets on the ramp can obviously see me, but many pretend they can't. I wonder whether or not I would pick myself up… I probably wouldn't…

The looks I do get from the passing drivers are confused, and sometimes surprised. One lady shakes her head at me, but it strikes me as a reaction of disbelief rather than disparagement.

Do Black people hitchhike? I wonder…

Two hours. Nobody pulls over. Nobody offers a ride. My first strikeout.

I get on the train and go back to my hotel. The shower feels good.

CHAPTER 13: BIRMINGHAM

Birmingham in White

The journey from Atlanta to Birmingham requires more poise and patience than I anticipated.

I've purchased a Greyhound ticket. I'm in Atlanta's bus depot with my bag, waiting in line at the customer service desk. The bus was supposed to leave at 9 AM, but it's 9:15 and I haven't heard any update. No announcements have been made.

The man behind the desk informs me the bus that was supposed to take us to Birmingham has been involved in an accident. A replacement bus will be around in a few hours, he alleges. He's a fat, angry-looking man. I don't interrogate him.

Not knowing how long "a few hours" is, I figure it's best to stick close to the station. Unfortunately for me, this part of Atlanta is pretty terrible. It's a stone's throw away from the Atlanta City Detention Center — which, as one might expect, also situates it in the heart of the city's bond office district. Excellent urban design.

And so the whole area is a big mess. And I pace back and forth in front of the bus depot, waiting, watching, wondering...

.... wondering how people can be led to lead such fucked-up lives...

There is a woman marching up and down Forsyth Street. She is rambling, incomprehensibly, to the entire neighborhood. In one hand, she holds a bottle of malt liquor and a lighter. In the other hand, she holds a crack pipe that she shakily lifts to her lips every few paces. Her steps are short and spasmodic. She walks the way you would expect someone to walk if they had consumed nothing but malt liquor and crack cocaine for the past 72 hours.

Oh, and she is not wearing any clothes, nor is she wearing any shoes. She is walking 20 yards up the street, turning around, and then walking 20 yards back, in the middle of traffic, swearing to nobody … completely naked. She has been doing this for nearly half an hour.

Cars honk when she gets in their way. She acts as if they do not exist.

A man in a Falcons jersey and baggy jean shorts who has just walked out of the depot is offended.

"AAWWwwww hellllllllllll nahhhhhh," he groans, shaking his head. "Shorty got her shit out in front da whole naybahood."

It's true... Shorty does. Other people who are idling around offer similar reactions.

"Someone get dis bitch some damn pants!"

"Her bare ass 'bout to get smoked by one dem cars!"

It is a chaotic place. The naked woman is the most lurid spectacle, but not by much.

Three men are arguing in front of a parked sedan a few yards from where I am standing. I can't quite make out what they're saying, but two of the men seem upset at the third. I think the dispute is drug-related. I think a deal went sideways. The two men begin shoving the third, and then punching him. He falls to the ground, bleeding profusely from the mouth. He manages to scamper away from them, toward the depot's doorway, but they follow. They grab him just before he gets into the building and continue punching him. Blood splatters all over the glass doors. The beating goes on for 30 or 40 seconds before a security officer comes out from the building and tells the two men to "Get the fuck off him!" Like most security guards in Georgia, he's carrying.

It's noon. I want to go back in and ask the fat, angry-looking information desk guy if there are any updates on the replacement bus, but the door is covered in blood.

Eventually, the replacement bus comes.

The actual bus ride is, thankfully, far less eventful than the station. There are no antics, just dismal chatter. The woman sitting in the row ahead of me tells another woman who is sitting across the aisle that she is going to Texas, which is a 19-hour journey. Two agitated toddlers are crawling on top of her. I lean back in my seat, looking at them, and tell myself I'm lucky that I haven't gotten anyone pregnant yet.

I don't actually get off in Birmingham. I get off a bit earlier in Anniston — partly because it seems like it has more accessible shoulders, and partly because it reduces the amount of time that I'm forced to spend alongside the other unfortunate Greyhound riders.

The city of Anniston holds a historical significance that most Americans don't know about…

On May 14th, 1961, five months before the publication of Griffin's *Black Like Me,* Anniston was the site of a dramatic confrontation between the opposing vanguards of America's racial war — a confrontation that would have national implications for the burgeoning Civil Rights Movement.

The event involved a Greyhound bus transporting a racially mixed group of activist Freedom Riders. Departing from Washington, the group had traveled through Virginia, the Carolinas, and Georgia as a means of testing a recent Supreme Court decision.

Specifically, the group's goal was to enforce the Supreme Court's ruling in *Boynton v. Virginia* (1960), which declared segregated facilities for interstate passengers illegal. Their journey targeted the prevailing Jim Crow laws in the South, which enforced racial segregation in the public facilities that made up interstate transit networks — structures like bus terminals, their shelters, restaurants, and waiting rooms.

As the bus arrived in Anniston, it encountered a mob consisting of Ku Klux Klan members and other outraged Alabamans who had been incited by law enforcement officials sympathetic to the Klan's racial ideology. These officials included Eugene "Bull" Connor, the infamous segregationist leader, a man who was the Birmingham Commissioner of Public Safety at the time.

A plaque at Anniston's Freedom Riders National Monument says that dozens of Klansmen encircled the bus while taunting the riders and brandishing improvised weapons: "The mob, carrying metal pipes, clubs, and chains milled around menacingly, some screaming 'dirty communists' and 'Seig Heil.'" They slashed the vehicle's tires, preventing it from continuing on to Birmingham, and then proceeded to set it on fire. Law enforcement, conspiring with Connor, let all of this happen. The passengers inside were temporarily trapped but eventually managed to escape, despite sustaining injuries.

The local and federal authorities' lack of proactive involvement raised questions about the role of systemic racism within law enforcement — questions that had not-so-mystifying answers. The lack of immediate police intervention during the assault, likewise, was a major point of public contention and criticism.[13]

The aftermath of the Anniston bus attack had far-reaching ramifications on America's racial discourse. Images of the burning bus circulated widely, bringing national attention to the severity of resistance against the Civil Rights Movement. The incident not only exposed the extreme levels of racial animosity in the South but also served to galvanize public support for integration, particularly in the North. The brash, brutal nature of the attack, in this otherwise dull and unassuming Alabama backwater, is often cited as a key factor in the Kennedy administration's move to take a more active role in addressing civil rights issues.

What happened in Anniston was a big deal.

I imagine that most of the Freedom Rides were painfully boring and uneventful. I imagine it was like hunting, fishing, or fighting a war — where the monotony seems to drag on forever. And then, frenziedly, the slow moment is interrupted by a moment of magic so overwhelming and devastating that all the waiting is justified. The few short hours in Anniston were that magic.

Anniston is a quiet place today. I don't see a single pedestrian on the downtown street of the Freedom Riders Monument.

The bus drops me off in a part of Anniston that is basically Oxford. The resulting confluence, according to Google Maps, is called Oxanna. I walk through town for an hour or so until I get to I-20.

Today's shoulder is halfway up a 300-yard on-ramp. It's a plain, boring area. There is nothing within a mile except for gas stations, fast food chains, and the sort of motels where you can still get a room for $70 a night. It's late in the afternoon. I wish it were later in the afternoon. It's 90 degrees out, and after 20 minutes on the side of the road, I start to feel all 90. I'm glad I'm White today.

I stand there with my arm out, thumb up, and watch the merging vehicles pass me by. There are so many trucks in this country. *Why? Why do so many Americans insist on owning 6,000-pound, 20-foot-long monsters? What's all the space for? Are you hauling stuff? Really? You need that whole bed? For lumber? Gravel? Bricks? Are you doing it for fun? I've driven trucks. It's not that fun. Are you doing it to get laid? Hmmmm…* But that doesn't explain why so many women have trucks…

I suppose Americans have trucks because they are *supposed* to. It's hot out, and I'm tired, and I decide that finding another justification isn't necessary.

An hour and three minutes go by. A gray truck pulls over. I notice a glaring absence of lumber, gravel, and bricks in the bed.

The driver is a middle-aged white man who looks like he could be my father. There are no passengers.

"Where to?"

"Atlanta."

He is going to Tuscaloosa. He tells me I'm on the wrong side of the road. I conjure up a little crumb of embarrassment.

And why did he stop for me? I ask, as I always do.

"Why did I stop?" he repeats. He seems confused by the question. "You're standing out here with your thumb up."

He stopped because he was *supposed* to. It's hot out, and I'm tired, and I decide that finding another justification isn't necessary.

Birmingham in Black

It's a few degrees hotter out today. I'm at the shoulder an hour or so earlier than yesterday, which means the sun is directly overhead. The Afro is big. It acts as a sort of ringleted parasol. Neither my neck nor my nose burn when I'm black.

The lighting in the motel bathroom was terrible, and so I'm more self-conscious than usual about how convincingly Black I am.

But there's no need to be self-conscious here. This isn't downtown Atlanta. Nobody sees me leave my room. When I make it to the shoulder, the only people who lay eyes on me are the people who are speeding by at 60 miles per hour.

The vehicles feel like they're speeding up the ramp faster today than they were yesterday.

Maybe that's fine. As a matter of law, they don't *need* to pick me up. As a matter of law, they don't *need* to lend a proverbial hand. As a matter of law, they don't *need* to be brotherly or sisterly. As a matter of fact, dreamland can't be legislated into existence — even if it can be spoken into existence as a matter of creed and conviction.

> *I have a dream: That one day, down in Alabama, with its vicious racists, with its governor having his lips dripping with the words of "interposition" and "nullification" — one day right there in Alabama little black boys and black girls will be able to join hands with little white boys and white girls as sisters and brothers!*

I wonder if King's devotees possessed a greater sense of moral clarity back then. I don't know what it means to be sisterly or brotherly in a country like this, at a time like this.

And as I stand here, my blackened thumb in the air, I wonder what percent of these drivers would pull over and offer me a ride if the federal government forced them to — if it enshrined the right of hitchhikers to be picked up into American law. Would these Alabamans acquiesce? Would they stop their trucks on the shoulder like good citizens, like good brothers, and like good sisters? I wouldn't be surprised if they interposed or nullified.

The two hours come to an end. I walk back to the motel.

It was a long, strange day.

I feel anxious and out of sorts in the Deep South. Back in my room, where the world is much smaller, I think about a passage Sprigle wrote from his time in Alabama:

> *We were seeking haven for the night in Huntsville, Alabama, where we were sure of lodging and food. As the miles dropped behind us, I realized that this whole thing was getting my nerve. A little after midnight we pulled into the Negro section of that northern Alabama town. Only once before in my life had I experienced the relief and comfort and sense of safety that I did when we unkinked ourselves from the car and joined those friendly black faces on the sidewalk. That was when, back in London in '40, I'd come up out of Southwark where the Germans had been pegging high explosive at us night after night, and I'd drop down into the air-raid shelter of the Waldorf, two stories underground.*

I take a shower. I wash the black off as best as I can. I take very deep breaths and find myself overcome by a sense of relief, comfort, and safety that feels not so different from the relief, comfort, and safety that met me in the mornings after long nights underneath the streets of Kyiv.

Air raids and transracialism, it seems, are two of man's eternal stressors.

CHAPTER 14: LOS ANGELES

Los Angeles in White

I order a cab to the corner of 6th and Olive. It's an interesting part of the city. I don't think there is a single person in Pershing Square who is as sober as I am. In theory, this place should be one of the most impeccably maintained areas in the entire American empire. In reality, it's something of a zoo. It's funny. More people should spend time in downtown LA. I think it would humble those who pride themselves as patriots. I think it would suck much of the wind from the sails of the average American exceptionalist.

I tell the driver to take me to the shoulder spot I've picked out on the coast. He does the thing that ethnic cabbies and Uber drivers often do where he switches the music to something he assumes I'll enjoy, something massively popular and stereotypically White, like Jason Aldean or Cher. This particular guy thinks I prefer Nirvana to the belligerently mixed Arab dance record he was previously listening to. He isn't wrong. I try to convince myself that the music selection of these drivers doesn't influence my tipping behavior. It probably does.

We take I-10 through Culver City and Santa Monica. The windows were all rolled up when I got in, but he let me roll mine down. I stick my arm out and let it hang against the side of the door.

My hair blows around in the wind. It gets all pushed and pulled and whirled around. I don't care. I know it will look fine. "ThAT's hAiR prIviLeGE," I imagine being lectured by one of the girls I went to grad school with. In my mind, her voice is so shrill. But I suppose she isn't wrong.

I arrive. The shoulder is good.

79 degrees — sublime weather.

42 minutes — a sublime wait time.

My saviors are two Millennial guys in an off-white sprinter van. They are both off-White in terms of complexion, though I'm sure they would describe themselves as White. I guess that applies to a lot of Whites in this country. They are *American Whites*…

I tell them that I'm trying to get to Santa Clarita in a straight shot. They look confused by this, obviously. They tell me they are going to Oxnard. I turn them down.

… but before they leave:

"Hey, by the way, why'd you guys pull over?"

The driver looks at the passenger, and then between the seats toward the back of the van… and then at me.

"We've got space."

America has oceans of space. Having space has never been the problem.

Los Angeles in Black

The contacts went in more easily than normal today. Maybe I'm getting the hang of it. Maybe engaging in transracialism is just like anything else: practice makes perfect. Maybe I could teach a workshop.

I leave the hotel and go back to the shoulder. Nobody bothers me on the way. Nobody asks me for anything. Despite feeling the imagined weight of surveilling glances, I can see through my artificially dark hazel eyes that far fewer people are looking at me today than yesterday. I am not invisible, *per se*, but I am more naturally a part of the urban gestalt. This is, I'm starting to realize, what it's like to be Black in the inner city.

It's 77 degrees and a little overcast — great hitchhiking weather. It would be sublime if I could get a ride soon, I think to myself, but waiting for the entire two hours wouldn't be horrible. I could use the fresh air.

The spot is waiting for me. I plant my feet. My thumb goes up.

It's a breezy day, and my mind is breezy.

Beach houses are blocking the view of the ocean, but I can hear the waves. I can smell the salt. The curls of my Afro caper and cavort in the soft wind. The muted sun casts an easy glow over my dark brown skin. My sunglasses are in my pocket so that my entire face can be seen by any oncoming motorist who cares to look. I am trying to appear approachable.

Convertibles race by one after another, as if they are late to the money convention. The cars seem nicer today than they did yesterday. They seem faster, shinier, and less capable of decelerating.

My thumb wiggles in the air, hoping to ensnare a kindred spirit, but the Bentley is too lost in its own dreamscape to notice. Then, a shadowy Lamborghini flits past, purring like a cosmic cat with a ball of tangled, stardust secrets. *Does it navigate by the constellations of capital?* I wonder…

The world around me becomes a carousel of distant whimsy and glitter. A Rolls-Royce saunters by, shimmering with an aura that smells of Tom Ford's Soleil Brûlant and enigmatic riddles. I tap my foot, humming.

Pick a Black man up?

Pick a Black man up today, king?

Pick a Black man up?

NO!!! No, no, no... That's not how this works. The strangers don't want you in their car, man. You could be dangeroussssssss. You could have a knife, or a gun, or a mean cross and a callous disregard for life.

One hour passes. The cars are so nice. Fuck.

Malibu money, I suppose... *But were they this nice yesterday?* I can't quite remember.

Two hours. No dice. A few accidental glances, but no "Whereareyaheaded?"s.

CHAPTER 15: LAS VEGAS

Las Vegas in White

"Uhhhh… That's on the outskirts of town," says the cab driver.

"It sure is," I reply, not having the slightest interest in telling him what I'm up to.

I don't take taxis very often, but the Uber pricing has been insane lately. And on Black days, of course, it isn't even an option because the Sam Forster who appears in my profile picture is White.

He drives me close to the spot on the interstate that I picked out on Google Maps.

It's not even eight, but the sun is already hammering the city. It's already so hot out. This may be the hardest shoulder.

The drive is short. We don't talk. I keep my glasses on until we arrive.

I get out of the car and walk a few hundred feet to a spot on the ramp that has a sizable shoulder. Inside my backpack are two liters of water, which I plan on spacing out evenly throughout the hundred and twenty minutes, should it actually take that long.

A dozen-odd vehicles pass. They look at me, pityingly, as they accelerate to highway speed. Or maybe their looks are neutral and the pity is my own imputation. Being on the side of a road while massive trucks fly by at 80 miles per hour makes you vulnerable, and that vulnerability breeds paranoia. It makes you feel like an ungainly newborn fawn, or like a woman.

When you're on the side of the road, you're only a slight twitch or jerk of the arm away from instant death. If a driver were overcome with the urge to kill you — even for a fraction of a second — they could… and probably, nobody would ever find out. The actual arm movement itself would be so trivial. It would all be so quick and easy… and painless. It would be like swatting a mosquito on your leg. One instant there would be life, and the next there wouldn't. Just a tiny turn of the wheel and **!SMACK!** . Total darkness.

The sun climbs in the sky. Beads of sweat ball themselves together on my forehead.

I don't like to have my sunglasses off when I'm outside, but it is important to have one's face unobscured. The eyes let people know you're a real human being and not a featureless killer. Plus, my face is exceptionally benign and disarming, or so I've been told.

37 minutes. Bingo. Jackpot. Lucky me. A white, one-ton pickup truck pulls over a hundred feet up the road. He and I had made a few seconds of solid eye contact as he passed by. Like Nashville, it's a work rig. He shouldn't be picking up strange men. Alas, this is Sin City, and over the course of the 12 hours since I've been here, I've developed the distinct impression that Nevadans follow rules like cats follow marching orders.

"Where are you trying to get?" He is a solidly built man a decade my senior. He's White.

"Reno."

"Reno? On this road?"

I shrug my shoulders.

"Nahh, I'm headed to Mesquite," he says.

"Ahh, well, I appreciate the offer…" I say. He gives a sympathetic nod. "And hey, I've been on this road for a while, and nobody has stopped. Why'd you pull over?"

"I like the company… and I also used to hitchhike a bit when I was a kid too."

A kid?!?! I decline the ride but accept the compliment, despite how obliquely and unintentionally it was given.

Las Vegas in Black

My pupils connect with themselves in the mirror's reflection. I am applying the dark foundation to my cheeks and forehead. Even after a few days' worth of experience, performing this transformation feels very bizarre.

What are you doing, Sam???

I put another dab of the foundation on and rub it in with the foam blender as the nagging uncertainty pushes itself in.

Is this too far? Is it too fucked up? Is this… is this good?   Is this a good idea?

The color is a bit spotty on my neck. I hit it with a pump of Maybelline to smooth things out.

Of course this is a good idea. You wouldn't do it if it wasn't one!

My thoughts are interrupted by the loud, cracking sound of palm against flesh coming from the hotel room next to me. A woman is groaning and grunting. She is, I presume, getting the sort of brutish and uncontrolled attention that she couldn't get outside of Vegas.

It's not an especially nice hotel that I'm staying in, but it is right on the strip. It's a slick, slimy, seedy, seventies-looking establishment. Everyone who is staying here has come with the express intent to debase themself.

As I listen to the woman next door getting railed by God-only-knows-who, I think about all of the bizarre incidents and encounters that have doubtlessly occurred in this very room. It's entirely possible that my racial transformation is not among the top ten strangest things that have gone on in 779 — and that possibility comforts me.

I ride the elevator down seven stories.

These people are animals. Walking through the casino floor, the lights are too bright. The sounds are too loud. It's all a blur of colors and faces. The air, thick with smoke, is suffocating, choking out any sense of sanity. Heartbreaking excuses for men and women, tethered to machines, feed themselves tirelessly, eyes glazed over in gluttonous obsession. Everywhere I look, the trappings of excess cling to them. Stomachs spilling over belts, nicotine-stained fingers hitting buttons, their faces weary and worn. Laughter here seems cruel, not joyful.

I hear the clink of coins; the false hope rings out of them. Everywhere, the weight of vice drags these 'people' down, permanently affixing them within our glowing neoliberal hellscape. This isn't the dream; it's the nightmare. *How did we get here?* God, if He ever visited, seems to have checked out.

This place, this modern America, is a testament to our loss of self, our loss of Him.

The ugliness is not just in the faces, but in the soul of this place. It's too much.

I do not feel paranoid as I make my way through the sea of zombies. They are preoccupied… In some important sense, **mindlessness precludes racial consciousness**.

Black people gamble. White people gamble. Asians… Native Americans… blah blah blah… The fruit machines don't care about race. I do not have the impression that anyone in the room cares about my Blackness. They are ABSORBEDDD in their games.....

I realize I am rambling, but the people at casinos truly do make me sick. What they are doing is gross. I want to emphasize this. The whole institution is a deeply woeful waste of life.

It's a shame that more people aren't self-aware. It's a shame that more people aren't directing their energy toward *meaningful* endeavors, like me. I fluff my Afro and walk out the front door.

I get a cab and head back to the spot. I have two liters of water. Today, I will probably end up drinking it all before heading back.

Stupid taxi chatter ensues, but he quickly and correctly picks up that I don't have strong feelings about the weather.

We arrive at the spot. I get out. The thumb goes up. A dozen cars pass. Then two dozen. Then I drink the first liter.

The sun gets higher in the desert sky. I wonder again whether my skin is more or less likely to burn under all the makeup.

I see a few familiar faces from yesterday. None of them make eye contact as they fly by. I seriously doubt they recognize me.

I don't think I look any younger or older; I just look Black. To them, I look as Black as any Black guy who has ever hitchhiked through Nevada... probably...

It's very hot. I wipe the sweat from my forehead, smearing some of the charcoal eyebrow pomade on the back of my hand.

An SUV slows down, and I think he's about to stop, but it turns out he is just an overly cautious merger. He gets on the interstate and, like everyone else, leaves me behind.

I finish the last bit of my water a minute or two before the two-hour mark. No dice.

CHAPTER 16: CHICAGO

Chicago in White

There are probably half a handful of American cities that have produced more than half a handful of truly famous writers. Chicago is one of those cities. Hemingway, Bradbury, Sandburg... Kanye... Chief Keef... You know most of these names, and there's a good chance your parents do too. That's a big deal.

It's a tall, loud, imposing city. It's effusive and intrusive and abusive. It's a nursery for good writing. It may be the closest thing to New York in the entire world. It's sort of like if New York were more believable... like if New York were real life...

But I do believe I'm the only decent writer on the train at the moment. In Chicago, good writers don't take the L.

We are going north from Midway. I get off the train and transfer to a different train that takes me to the southern suburbs. The trip is about an hour.

I walk a mile from the station to a spot on the side of an interstate on-ramp. It has a healthy shoulder and a long lead before the merge. I believe that what I'm doing is probably illegal. As is the case in most states, the hitchhiking laws in Illinois leave much to the discretion of law enforcement.

In any case, there's enough of a ditch that I think I could convince a cop that I'm simply out picking up garbage. I doubt any cop would be stupid enough to actually believe that, but I bet it would be one of those statements that is accepted for the sake of mutual convenience despite being an obvious lie.

The sky is overcast, and the air is exactly room temperature. It's perfect weather for idling. I think this is the best spot yet. I start my timer.

It's late in the afternoon. The traffic is light. A procession of trucks pass by — then a camper van with a rusted-out bumper. Most of the people look like farmers. Some of the drivers smile at me. They don't let themselves nod, but at least their looks are free of the contempt that lathered the faces of the drivers in previous locations. It's also striking how much friendlier these people seem than the people on the train. Nobody scowls at me like they did on the train. Things are very different out here, even though I am only a dozen miles or so from the city limits.

It's peaceful. The edge of rural Illinois isn't so bad. I could wait for a while.

But I don't… 28 minutes in, a middle-aged man in a red minivan pulls over.

I approach the open passenger-side window. He looks like one of my little league baseball coaches. His name could be "Hank," "Gus," or "Ted." He's alone, but the back seats are filled up with cardboard U-Haul boxes.

"Where ya' trying to get to?"

"Indianapolis."

"Indy? All the way out here?"

"Yeah," I reply, confidently.

He is not going to Indianapolis… obviously.

He is going to Champaign. I decline the ride.

Why did he stop? I ask him.

"I told God I would start doing more good deeds," he responds. He seems like the sort of character who I'd like to catch a ride with to Champaign.

Then again, why would I go to Champaign?

Chicago in Black

I leave my hotel and head toward the train station. I am a Black man on the south side of Chicago. I feel extremely uncomfortable, but I do believe that I blend in. The same way that a towering, blonde-haired Dane blends in on the streets of Copenhagen, the same way a bearded, thawb-wearing Arab man blends in on the streets of Riyadh, I blend in here.

I haven't seen much of the city, so I decide to go for a walk before getting on the commuter train that will take me to the section of shoulder I visited yesterday.

I go through Bronzeville and Washington Park. The cityscape decays. There is garbage and rotting food strewn out across the sidewalks. The air smells gross. It's baffling to think that one of the world's most prestigious universities is just a few blocks away.

Each step feels crushingly light. The buildings, which were perhaps tall and proud in the distant past, show signs of crumbling. The empty lots are overgrown. They stretch out like gaps in a crooked smile. *Hmmmm... yes.* People told tales of its danger, and the gaps seem to confirm it. *Why else would these spaces remain void in such an important city?*

Old men sit on rickety benches and look at me as I walk. Their eyes are murky. Children play — some on basketball courts, but more on their phones. They say things that I can understand, but that I couldn't possibly transcribe. They yell for reasons that I don't quite comprehend. The very air feels stifled, like the city itself is struggling to breathe here. This is Chicago. There is much more of this flavor of Chicago than there is of the flavor that's advertised in the airport travel brochures.

The weight of neglect is palpable. Everything that's gross and ugly reads like a story of hopeless desperation. I walk fast. I tread cautiously. I feel like an intruder in a world where life fights a ceaseless grapple with death. Trudge. Trudge. Trudge. Trenchwork.

I walk along Martin Luther King Drive. I wonder how many Martin Luther King Drives exist in this nation. Then I wonder where this one ranks among them. It's pretty ugly. Then again, most of them are. I know that it's a massive cliché to point this out, but it is sort of wild how reliably MLK is forced to share his name with a city's most dreadful roadway. It's almost as if these cities are all making a humorous overture to the grave — as if to derisively let him know that his great dream never materialized.

I continue to walk. I make it to the infamous Parkway Gardens — "O Block" as it's often referred to by the generation that grew up with YouTube. Like most Cuspers who listen to rap, I know about this place. I've heard about it thousands of times.

I distinctly remember watching Chief Keef music videos back when he was first blowing up in 2012. I remember thinking that he was 20 years older than me. He's actually one year older than me. Walking around O Block and observing the neighborhood's abrasive features does a great deal to demystify why that 16-year-old boy gave me the impression that he was a grown man. Lifespans are shorter in the projects. The milestones of maturation, if you can call them that, are markedly accelerated. According to the internet, he already had at least one kid at that point. I think I was still a few months away from getting on base. Different worlds.

I walk on the sidewalk parallel to pointed iron gates that partition the project's housing units from West Woodlawn. It's entirely unclear to me why these gates exist. It's unclear to me what purpose they serve other than to make the place feel more bleak and unsettling. In the colloquial sense, a "gated community" is one that employs physical exclusion as a means of social engineering. Gates are built and maintained to keep the rabble out. And maybe such communities are pompous and elitist, but at least their gates reflect a sort of practical logic.

I am not struck by the same practical logic as I walk alongside the O Block gates. *Are they meant to keep people out?* I try to imagine the people who require a barrier to be kept away from these dreary, dirty, low-rise heaps of brick — arguably some of the gravest architectural sins of Modernism.

Maybe the gates are meant to help reduce crime? I suppose gates are less of a hassle for politicians than law enforcement...

The projects remind me of the projects that pepper Brooklyn. They're all so ugly. They're all so offensive to the urban ideals that Chicago and New York are meant to represent. The philistines who run our governments are always droning on about the housing crisis, blabbing about the need to build as many units as possible, as quickly and cheaply as possible. This is a loser mindset, and I don't know why it's tolerated. I lament how it reduces the matter of our inhabited spaces to a matter of blunt economic metrics. I wonder why powerful people insist that we must have a certain number of ugly buildings designated for poor people. *Why can't all of the buildings just be nice? Why must everything be subordinated to the cult of efficiency?*

I know that I promised this book would be descriptive, not normative, but I can't help myself on matters of physical beauty. Here, I know that my desire to judge makes me worse at describing the way things are, but this impulse is extremely powerful. I often feel like the monitor that I observe the world through is four or five notches brighter than the monitors of everyone else around me.

I think that's why I'm writing this. I think that's why you're reading this.

I meander the area for a few minutes. I continue walking. I approach a group of teenage boys who are idling on the street corner, smoking weed. Three of them are wearing hoodies with the hoods up. A fourth boy is wearing a Gucci t-shirt. One girl (noticeably younger than the boys) stands next to them as she eats some sort of specialty-flavored Skittles. They're all listening to a drill instrumental on a Bluetooth speaker.

One of the hooded boys begins to freestyle to the music as I pass by.

It is funny to me that the universe exists in such a way that has pressured him and I toward the same occupation: just dicking around with words. We're both just trying to convert experienced phenomena into letters and sounds that make the world comprehensible, both to ourselves and to those around us...

What if I hopped in? Would it be the worst thing in the world if we did it together? No, no, no. I classify that temptation alongside the urge to reach for an officer's gun: keep it purely fantastical.

I do sometimes wish I was more musically gifted. I write verse well, but coupling lyrics with melodies has never been my thing. I think about how I probably would have been a drill rapper if I were to have been born Black in Chicago's South Side. Like this teen, I would probably be transforming O Block's sights and sounds and tastes into words that I would yell over an aggressive, crudely produced instrumental. I'd probably have an ego about it. I'd probably try my best to leverage it as a crutch to get pussy.

The one girl has her hand on the thigh of the freestyler. She's leaning into him. The other boys are just standing there with hand-devoid thighs.

There's a big lesson in there.

I keep walking. I'm relieved that the boys don't say anything to me. They barely glance at me as I pass by.

The previous night, when my skin was white, I had an encounter with a similar group of teens outside a Chipotle that went quite differently. I had been walking along, minding my own business when one of them aggressively started asking me for money, and then swearing at me when I refused to give him any.

"Ayo, you fuckin' trippin'. Fuck you and yo mamma, nigga — witchya pasty bitch ass."

Black teenagers using "nigga" as the default pronoun, regardless of the race of the subject, is actually pretty common. I suspect a lot of foreigners and people who live outside of cities would be surprised to learn this. I've personally been called "nigga" by black people hundreds if not thousands of times in my life….. Which is kind of interesting… Sure, I'm more inculcated in the culture than most Whites, but probably only by one or two standard deviations — nothing crazy.

I couldn't help but notice that all of the teens outside this Chipotle had iPhones and designer clothes. I wonder if they would have left me alone had they encountered the version of me that exists today — the Black version.

I decide to leave O Block and head to the commuter station that will take me out of the city for the day's hitchhiking attempt. I've already been walking for a long time, and I anticipate having to spend the full two hours on the shoulder once I get there.

The train ride is quiet and uneventful. Commuting culture is not doing so hot in Chicago. I get to the terminus and then march the mile back to the spot on the interstate shoulder where I stood yesterday.

I start the timer and wait. I notice how, unlike yesterday's drivers who seemed to offer a stream of friendly glances, today's look straight forward and pretend not to notice me. Whether I'm in front of pedestrians on the sidewalk or in front of motorists on the road, I seem less likely to be ignored when my skin is White than when it's Black, as it is today.

Of course, it's impossible not to notice me, a tall Black man with a big Afro in broad daylight, standing in what is essentially farmland...

A police car approaches, but I see him from relatively far away, and I quickly put my thumb down.... I turn around and walk in the direction of the road, making sure to be well off the actual roadway. I hear the car getting nearer. I worry about what will happen if he questions me and asks for ID... Naturally, I have no interest in explaining why the face on my driver's license looks nothing like the face on my head today.

The officer drives by without slowing down. Lucky me.

Once the car is out of sight, I pace back to my spot. I'm tired from the big walk through the South Side. I want to go home...

Two hours elapse. No takers. Nobody wants me riding shotgun today.

I walk back to the train and then go straight back to the hotel.

I'm very thirsty, but I decide to take the makeup off before pouring myself a glass of water. It seems like it doesn't come off as easily today.

I walk to the window of my hotel room and stare eastward across Lake Michigan. A White face with faint traces of brown makeup at its periphery stares back at me in the reflection of the window. It's so surreal.

CHAPTER 17: DETROIT

Detroit in White

"Scu'me, sir. Got a dolla'?"

His clothes, presumably once of color, are now a faded patchwork, fraying at the edges and stained with memories of a very distant yesterdecade. His skin is ashen and dirty. Eyes hollow, unfocused. Hair unwashed. Fingers twitching all over the place.

There are open scabs everywhere.

They punctuate his dark skin, reminiscent of a tarnished constellation map on an ebony sky. Their appearance varies. Some are fresh, crimson and raw; others aged, crusted like dried riverbeds. They are juxtaposed against the veins, some bulging and others collapsed.

"I'm just tryna' get summthin' to eat," he tells me.

I look at the wounds, and my mouth fills up with the tart taste of loose change. It's like I'm gargling a handful of pennies.

I don't answer him. Whether or not I have cash doesn't even cross my mind. *What am I going to do, give him money?* It would be ridiculous to do something like that. I might as well get a pocketknife and cut out the next chunk of flesh for him. That would save time.

I think about all of the people I know and love who would, as a matter of instinct, actually take the time to wonder whether or not they have cash to give. These people are almost always suburbanites.

I have been walking from the bus station for a minute or two at most. I just arrived on the Greyhound from Chicago. It was a fine ride. I think I could be convinced to live in Ann Arbor, but probably not Kalamazoo. The penultimate stop was in Southfield, which meant coming into the city from the north… which meant crossing Eight Mile Road…

"Eight Mile" is a great song. I listened to it as I sat on the bus. Some of the lyrics are especially resonant. I did that thing where I leaned my head against the window, staring at the cars on the freeway without blinking while pretending that I'm in a music video. I mean, in some sense I am the guy from the movie. I'm out here writing, battling, creating — and the world just doesn't understand. Nobody understands except me…

But instead of writing lyrics on a bunched-up ball of paper during my commute to the bumper factory, I'm using my phone's notes app to write the manuscript for an experimental work of literary non-fiction that could completely derail my career and thoroughly fuck up every aspect of my life. It could ruin me. I'm writing something that will turn me into a target, but I believe I'm doing it extremely well...

Spiritually, and in every other way that matters, it's basically the same thing. I'm basically the guy from the movie.

Why do I put up this fight? Why do I still write?

But I'm still white, sometimes I just hate life

So I must then get off the bus, then split

Mhmmmmmmm…. Yessssss…… Very much yes. There is a profound energy here.

Circumstance, every now and then, will assign White men to Black spaces. The experience is psychologically powerful. In many cases, it engenders a sense of resentment and insecurity. And in many cases, this resentment and insecurity leads to a defiance that scares the mainstream. White guys in Black spaces are pugilists. They are irreverent. They do not abide by White norms. They do not seek the approval or adulation of 'White' institutions. They will say what they want to say. They will GO OFF with total abandon. Back when Eminem was who he really is, he would say whateverrrrrrrrr.

It's just me bein' me; here, want me to tone it down? Suck my ███████*, you* █████*! You happy now?*

These days, not even black rappers will say "███████"!

Maybe cash is the strongest bleach. In any case, Eminem doesn't start talking like this if he grows up White, and he doesn't stop were it not for the money. Hundreds of millions of dollars will do that, apparently.

It's all relative though, which means I'm ███████ than a lot of the ██████ who will have a problem with this book.

I imagine that Eight Mile is less of a meaningful socioeconomic partition than it was 20 years ago, but there was still a stark change in scenery when my bus crossed over the road. Detroit proper remains a very typical example of urban decay. Despite efforts at gentrification, there is an unmistakable sense of cultural anemia, and of general hopelessness. The right people are not bullish on Detroit. It feels like nobody important wants this place to win.

Some people try, of course, but it takes more than a smattering of electric scooters and exposed-brick gastropubs to undo half a century of dereliction.

I continue walking. I come across another junkie — this time a woman.

She is leaning against a chain-link fence. Her frame is thin, almost skeletal. Puffy lips contrast with flat, bag-circled eyes. The rough wear of vagrant life marks her everywhere, obscuring her real age. Maybe she's my age. Maybe we graduated high school in the same year. I wonder if she graduated at all.

She bites at her nails. She looks up at me, about to speak, but I hit her with my most solemn glance, and she closes her mouth before the request for money can spill out. She's pretty, in her own way. It's soul-crushing to see such a raging waste of life.

I wonder what she looked like ten years ago. I wonder if I would have wanted to fuck her back then. I wonder what she will look like ten years from now…I wonder if a future version of me would ever want to fuck her. Many terrible turns would have to be taken, I figure. Thinking about that makes me feel ill. I'm glad I haven't eaten today.

It's a sad city. Then again, I expected it to be a sad city… …
…

In the early 20th century, Detroit was the very embodiment of American industrial might and innovation. As the birthplace of the modern automotive industry, the city was a hub of feverish activity and skyrocketing prosperity. Factories buzzed around the clock, producing iconic vehicles that transformed American roads and revolutionized transportation worldwide. This Motor City, as it proudly came to be known, attracted waves of domestic and international migrants, all in search of the vaunted American Dream. The bustling streets echoed with the sounds of commerce, jazz music, and the multilingual chatter of its diverse, multiethnic populace. Architectural marvels rose, reflecting the city's opulence, from the majestic Detroit Opera House to the ornate Guardian Building. Entrepreneurial spirit thrived in tandem with a burgeoning middle class. Cultural institutions flourished. The city was considerably more than a manufacturing powerhouse; it was a beacon of culture, innovation, and opportunity. Detroit's meteoric rise in the early decades of the 20th century showcased it as a center of promise. It was a testament to what human ingenuity and relentless drive could achieve. Last century was, in many ways, a golden era, with the potential of Michigan's metropolis seemingly boundless.

Deindustrialization, racial strife, and gross municipal mismanagement have since served as the biggest ice cream scoop to ever hollow out a major American city. The frosty pail of Motown that once held 1.85 million now holds under 650,000.

All of this is evident from the scenery...

It's time to test the generosity. It's time to see who will bestow upon me an act of micro-philanthropy as I prop myself up on the shoulder.

I take a taxi to an on-ramp a half hour from downtown. I hand the driver a wad of bills and step out.

The air is refreshing. I like the temperature. The slight yellowing of the leaves is nice. I think it's the first sign of autumn I've seen this year.

Cars, trucks, and vans get on the highway without me. I'm tired and want to get this over quickly. I try to smile and look friendly. My right hand is outstretched with an upward thumb. I use the other hand to rub against my clean-shaven face. I look significantly younger now than I do with facial hair, and I figure the neoteny renders me less threatening, more inviting.

An hour and nine minutes pass before a guy in a black Jeep SUV pulls over on the side of the ramp. He's probably 40. White.

"Where are you going?"

"Ann Arbor."

"Oh," he responds. He sounds disappointed, as if he were genuinely looking forward to having a passenger. That disappointment is confirmed when, upon being asked, he divulges that the reason he pulled over is because he enjoys the company.

The tragic thing about hitchiking's demise in North America is that there are so many millions of people who have to drive long distances by themselves on a regular basis. There are unknowable numbers of people behind the wheel — Black, White, Asian, and Latino — who want someone to riff with while they drive. Usually, these people are men, and usually, they are far lonelier than they will ever admit. For every one driver who gets murdered by a hitchhiker, I bet there are a thousand whose loneliness leads them to suicide.

I deprive the lone Michiganian of my company and take a cab back into Detroit's core.

Detroit in Black

Two of the men on the canvas in front of me are depicted cheating the third out of money. They are sitting around a wooden table upon which there is a grouping of cards, coins, and banknotes. I know most of this because the artist did a good job, and I know the rest because I can read the small label that accompanies the piece. The fourth man, the scene's only Black man, is sequestered in the corner of the room. The Black man is not at the table. From the fraught expression on his face, I get the sense that the Black man knows what's going on — or at the very least, that *something* is going on.

I'm looking at *The Card Players*, 1846, by Richard Caton Woodville. It's one of the smaller paintings in the Detroit Institute of Arts' American wing, but I feel pulled toward it.

I look around the gallery. The attendants are invariably Black. The visitors are invariably White. My eyes return to the painting. I feel the creeping urge to analogize, and the urge becomes overwhelming...

I think most of the people in the gallery are the cheated guy that I see on the canvas. I think some of the people in the gallery are the cheaters. And I am quite positive that some of them are the Black guy huddling in the corner.

I don't think there are many people who could accurately tag themselves. This country is a fucking mess, and few of us have any semblance of self-awareness.

Land of the free, home of the brave, etc., etc., etc...

On the cab ride to the shoulder, I catch a glimpse of my Afro in the reflection of my phone. My short sideburns make me self-conscious. I suspect that the cab driver might notice that I'm wearing a wig if he looks long enough, or closely enough. Luckily, I'm in the backseat.

And probably, I'm worrying for no reason. *What is this guy going to think?*

Hey, something is off about this passenger... hmmmmm.... Yeah, there's just something that's slightly off about the way he looks... I can't quite put my finger on it...

WAIT!? is this Black guy actually a White guy disguising himself as a Black guy?

But the driver says nothing... Of course he doesn't. It would be absurd for anyone to come to that conclusion going off of nothing but my appearance.

Who would do that? Who would challenge my Blackness? No... it seems totally out of the question. What I'm doing is so ridiculous and implausible that I am essentially above suspicion. Aside from my now-practiced application of makeup, my best cover is the reality of social expectation.

The worst-case scenario is that the cabbie thinks I'm just a normal Black guy who happens to be wearing a wig for whatever reason.

I arrive back at the spot on the side of the road. I start the timer and stick my thumb up.

I am tired. I think this might be the hardest thing I've ever had to do for a writing project.

Maybe the stuff in Ukraine was harder. Or maybe I just tolerated it better because I knew it would be seen as good work — if only by the segment of the population who want the war to end.

Conversely, I don't know if anyone other than me will think that writing this book is good. So far, I have told two people: one who I am legally obligated to tell, and one who I would tell even if I were legally obligated not to.

I think about the highways in Ukraine… I think about how many hours I would have to wait before someone would offer a ride to the Black version of me on the side of the road in Zaporizhzhia or Dnipro. Thinking about this kills 15 minutes. Trying to recall how many Black people I saw in Ukraine kills another 15. I believe the answer is four.

The remaining 90 minutes are uneventful.

I think about the painting a bit more, and about Detroit's art museum...

A decade ago, when the city was in the throes of its financial collapse, the museum's fate wasn't clear. It survived because clever, caring people made difficult deals known as the *Grand Bargain*.

In 2013, Detroit declared the largest municipal bankruptcy in U.S. history, a dire consequence of prolonged mismanagement. This economic turmoil brought the city to a crossroads where its cultural soul and fiscal responsibilities collided.

Central to this drama was the art museum, which is actually home to some of the most impressive works in the country. A lot of people don't know just how impressive Detroit's collection is. It punches way above its weight. Cézanne, Bruegel, Matisse, Monet, Munch, Redon, Rembrandt, Picasso, Van Gogh — it really does have a lot of world-class pieces.

As the city grappled with debt, these treasures became targets for creditors, people who saw the potential sale of the art as a means to reclaim millions owed. The prospect of auctioning off the DIA's collection posed a profound moral quandary: *Should a city sell off parts of its communal cultural heritage in order to satisfy financial obligations?*

In the midst of this crisis, a novel solution, the Grand Bargain, emerged. It was a complex plan designed to balance the scales of financial duty and cultural preservation. The deal involved raising $816 million from private foundations, DIA donors, and the state of Michigan. This fund, managed by the Foundation for Detroit's Future, was to be dispensed over 20 years, primarily to bolster underfunded city pensions, thereby easing the fiscal toll on Detroit.[14]

This arrangement narrowly averted the need to liquidate the DIA's art collection. More importantly, it sparked a broader debate about communalism and the role of public assets in society. It underscored the intrinsic value of publicly owned art, not just as a financial asset, but as a cornerstone of communal identity and shared cultural experience.

And so **maybe** this country is not **only** about the dispossessed getting cheated at every turn…

*The fact that the DIAs' collection remains available to the public — rather than being shrouded away in some private penthouse or villa — is proof that America's dispossessed aren't **always** cheated by the cunning financial elite, right?*

Well, the dispossessed don't really visit museums. Plus, there's no such thing as a free lunch, especially not when you break bread with the breed of monster who needs his name immortalized in marble. *How many billions of dollars, in the city of Detroit alone, have been legally kept beyond the reach of the taxman by these people?* If you know anything about the art world, you know that rich people use it as a glitzy, voguish means of legitimizing fortunes that have been amassed in ways that would make the soul-possessing layperson's skin crawl.

That world feels endlessly far away from the shoulder I'm standing on.

I try counting cars again, but I give up after a dozen or so. I think that getting a ride offer the first day as a Black man in Nashville was a bit of a fluke.

It's a long two hours.

I get a cab back downtown. I'm done being Black, done being ignored. I don't wait to get back to my Air BnB to transition back to being White. I slip into a cafe bathroom on Congress Street and scrub all of the black off my face and hands with a dozen makeup wipes that I've stashed in my backpack over the preceding two weeks.

Seven shoulders down.

CHAPTER 18: BLACK STROLLING

It's not as though I teleported to each of the shoulders. I had to travel there. On half of the days, that meant traveling throughout America's cities as a Black man. And while I relied on taxis quite a bit, I also did a decent amount of strolling.

Because I don't know anyone else in America who has earnestly spent time as both a White man and as a Black man, I believe it's worth sharing a few thoughts about the unequal social treatment that finds Whites and Blacks.

The social exercise of being perceived as a Black man in America is obviously different in a number of important ways from the social exercise of being perceived as a White man. The poignant rhetoric about women clutching their purses whenever they're near you — and crossing the street so as not to end up near you in the first place — may or may not be true. I suspect it's mostly true, but I also suspect that the extent of its truth is more closely tethered to variables like haircut, clothing, age, and tattoo coverage than the bleeding-heart BLM types would care to admit. I didn't experience any of that stuff in my (admittedly brief) time as a Black man, but I also didn't look like a gangbanger. Take that for what it's worth.

… There is, however, one acute observation I made that strikes me as being a clearer indictment of this nation's disparate racial experiences...

Homeless people don't behave the same way towards White and Blacks…

The most striking and reliable difference between walking around in America as a White man and walking around in America as a Black man is the frequency with which you are propositioned for money by the homeless.

I have, of course, spent many years walking around America's cities as a White man — particularly Dallas and New York, but I've also been to virtually every major American city. And in all of these places, as a White man, I am breathlessly and unendingly asked for money by homeless people. White homeless people, Black homeless people, Latino homeless people — all of them ask me for money… ALLLLLLLLLLLL the time. It doesn't stop.

And I walk past them as if they don't exist, or I offer a subtle, sympathetic shake of the head if I happen to commit the grave sin of eye contact.

They see what I look like, and they figure there's a decent chance I'll have cash, and they figure there's a smaller but not insignificant chance that I'll acquiesce, and so they feel comfortable asking, and so they ask.

Not a single homeless person asked me for money when I was Black.

And in some strange way, I almost felt less guarded around the homeless when I was Black. I felt as though I could offer a cordial glance or nod of the head without the fear of opening myself up to solicitation. If this phenomenon is indeed a broader reality, it surely has a profound impact on the texture of urban life, a domain wherein Blacks and the homeless are both drastically disproportionate.

CHAPTER 19: FINDING SHOULDER RACISM

If we lived in a world where White men and Black men were equally likely to be picked up while hitchhiking from the shoulders of America's highways, the chances that the White man would be picked up first at all seven shoulders would be less than 1%. Such an outcome would, in this hypothetical world of evenly distributed probability, occur in one out of every 128 experiments.

Now, it is entirely possible that this book represents the innocuous and statistically excusable one out of 128 outcomes that could have been. It's entirely possible that if I were to perform this experiment and write this book another 127 times, the White version of myself would not be so consistently fortunate.

But less than 1% is a small value...

Randomness doesn't strike me as the most likely explanation for what I experienced: seven rides offered as a White man versus one as a Black man, with the latter taking longer to get.

What seems much more likely is that the Black man I became was discriminated against. For whatever reason, he was seen as a less deserving or desirable passenger. Time and time again, he was subjected to the sort of soft, inconspicuous **shoulder racism** that emanates from all Americans, regardless of color, and that manifests without criticism or consequence.

Oftentimes, I'm sure, it manifests without notice at all.

PART THREE: SHOULDERS EVERYWHERE AND NOWHERE

CHAPTER 20: ON RACIAL CONSCIOUSNESS

There are other proverbial shoulders in American life, of course — not just the literal ones on the sides of highways. There are other situations where goodwill or indifference can freely be shown toward a person, based at least in part on race, without the risk of social reprisal.

Like all forms of racism, the perception of these shoulder scenarios is dependent on the recognition of racial identity. It relies on a person being cognizant of race, and cognizant of how racial identity may influence the perceptions of others.

Even in situations where someone is not actually subjected to discriminatory racial bias — which is to say, in situations where their race is not something that other people think or care about — it matters whether or not they *believe* they are subjected to discriminatory racial bias …

Belief matters because this perceived assessment will shape their worldview. It will immutably form their axioms about how the world works. And the more powerful the person is, the more expansively their perceptions reverberate throughout society. Identitarian causes are championed by identitarians. People who feel race is significant lead their lives accordingly… they manage accordingly… they govern accordingly…

And so, in order to truly understand American race relations, it is necessary to understand the racial consciousness of different racial groups. This consciousness, shaped by history and experience, dictates not only how groups interact but also how they perceive and react to societal structures. Just as a river is shaped by the terrain it flows through, so too are the thoughts and behaviors of people shaped by the consciousness of their race within the broader expanse of society.

What race are you? Is it something that is an important feature of your identity? Is it something you think about often? Do you care? Are you encouraged to tell people that you care? Are you influential? If so, do you induce your followers to care?

If the matter of American race relations is to be meaningfully grasped, so too must be the matter of attachment to racial identity within America.

As it so happens, a lot of Black people are honest about this sort of thing…

The two interviews that follow are instructive of what I mean when I reference "the matter of attachment to racial identity." I've spoken to many Black leaders, and an overwhelming majority of them share the views of my interviewees. There are plenty of other interviews that I could have showcased, but these two are fairly representative. They offer what I consider to be a well-embraced, middle-of-the-road perspective within the Black community.

The first interview is with a sitting US congressman. The second is with the mayor of a major American city. I've redacted identifying information because I don't want them to be associated with the book if they'd rather not be. As you might've guessed, I didn't volunteer any information about my use of journalistic blackface when I reached out for an interview...

The Congressman

1. How central is Blackness to your own personal identity?

It's an essential part of my identity. Blackness is essential to who I am for a series of reasons: 1. We'll start with my origins. I'm the son of ▮▮▮▮▮▮▮▮▮▮▮▮▮▮▮▮▮▮▮▮▮▮▮ ▮▮▮▮▮▮▮▮▮▮▮ — but make no mistake, I exist in my context of the state of the world as a Black man. There is no optionality when it comes to how I am seen in the world, and frankly, how I choose to be seen. I don't think that the concept of Blackness is able to be reduced to one set of experiences. In fact, I think the fact that it is dynamic is what makes it unifying across people with different origin stories. Whether or not it's coming to this country through forced migration, the enslavement of people from West Africa — ███████ ████████████████████████████ — we are united. Whether it's people from the Caribbean, who have an experience that is anchored in a similar version of struggle, but where there has historically been marginal differences in outcomes.

So, I say all of that because I view myself as a Black person through and through, and that is part of why I am able to serve the people of ██████████ It's part of how I will serve, and it's part of what I hope I am able to keep in my frame of reference as I continue to do this work as an elected official.

2. What do you see as the most challenging aspect of the Black experience in modern America?

Look, I would say that the most challenging experience for the community is a commitment to being aligned in our pursuit of the objectives that I think we're all seeking — which is economic opportunity, which is a reduction in health disparities, which is also making sure that the generation that follows has more ability to thrive than the one that came before it.

So, where we sometimes get stuck is how we're going to get there. It's always been that question, right? It's always been that question, you know, whether it was the disparities between Kingian non-violence and a more militaristic approach of the Black Power movement, whether it is rejection of Democratic Party politics or an embrace of the politics that has achieved so much for us. It is imperfect and still has a range of deficiencies in meeting the moment so that Black people can have the opportunities that they deserve. So, you know, that's okay. They say that without struggle there is no progress. That applies internally to people who share an identity about how they want to achieve their objectives. I often hear, "Government is not going to save us," but I do know the thing that has been the most effective in recent memory has been a set of committed actors, particularly Black leaders, who have helped move the Democratic Party, moved Congress, and decided multiple presidencies. That has resulted in things like the childhood poverty rate being cut for Black children because of an expanded Child Tax Credit. That doesn't just happen in the absence of Black voices. In fact, it is because of an understanding of how to service the needs of a community that it emerges.

So, the tactics may be different, but the goals are the same. We just have to be okay with there sometimes not being a one-size-fits-all approach to solving our most intractable problems, and meeting the moment on the brightest opportunities in the future.

** end of interview **

The Mayor

1. How central is Blackness to your own personal identity?

Well, Sam, frankly, it's who I am. I think about culture. I think about family. Those facets of my life are tied to the Black experience. I think about my professional life. I think about my personal life. Those are also tied to the Black experience.

My family — my █████████ and my ████ — raised me to treat others the way you'd want to be treated, and that their skin color did not matter.

I was always confused by why, for some reason, my skin color mattered to others.

I learned that at a very young age because I went to school in an area of the state where I was, at times, the only Black kid in the class. So, you knew you were Black where I went to school because you could walk into a room and immediately know how many Black people there were. I think that in those situations, you become very accustomed to being the only one — or one of a few.

I never saw my race as something that was an impediment, but I also always knew that there were people out there who were selling me short. And so, I embraced being the underdog. I embraced being overlooked and discounted.

As I grew up, and as I went to college, I came to understand that Blackness isn't homogeneous. There is a diversity to who we are. When you're a poor kid growing up in a White community, you have a very difficult time seeing that. But when you start to matriculate through higher education, and you're in rooms with others who are like you, but come from different families with a different socioeconomic status, you start to realize, oh, wow, there are doctors and lawyers and educators, and this is not just something in a book. This is real.

When I got to college, I set out to create a life like the ones I saw in the books — like those of lawyers, doctors, and other professionals.

I don't know how else to identify or explain how personal Blackness is to me. I live it every day. Sometimes it's hard to express to those who don't live in my shoes what I experience, what I see. There are microaggressions, and there are folks who just show straight-up aggression at times.

You like to think that these things are not because of the color of your skin — but when you experience enough, when you see enough, you start to open your eyes even wider.

2. What do you see as the most challenging aspect of the Black experience in modern America?

What's very obvious is a word that some are afraid to use, a word that some are afraid to talk about. It's the original sin of this country. It's called racism. That's the real challenge to being Black in America. And here's the thing: many of us in the Black community don't wake up in the morning to seek out racism. It's unfortunate but true that racism finds us.

I know that there are folks who are my detractors and naysayers who may claim, "All ████ does is just wake up in the morning wanting to talk about race." That's the furthest thing from the truth.

But I preside over a city that, unfortunately, has the issue of race in its bones.

I don't seek it out, but it certainly knows where I am. It knows my location. It knows what time I'm doing something. That is the most challenging part of my experience.

And it shows up in many different ways. It arrives on my doorstep in terms of a trope, a stereotype. People have lower expectations for some odd reason even though I have the same college diploma that they have.

It's interesting that it just seems to appear in opportune and inopportune times. That is truly the real challenge.

However, what I think that some people don't recognize is that, boy, it can really be a motivator as well.

When someone sets low expectations for me, when someone attempts to stereotype me because of some racist idea that has been put in their head, I love proving them wrong. I've done it most of my life. But the question is: should a person with the color of my skin have to work so hard to prove someone with this idea wrong? Believe it or not, we've been doing it for over 400 years in this country.

I have to say, despite these ideas that are poisonous, despite the impediments and barriers that have been set up before us, despite true challenges, many of us have excelled.

In my work, I try my best to create an environment in which my little girl can excel even if the ideas of racism may be in her path. I'm going to set her up for success. I've done that, and I want to continue to do that for every kid who looks like me — because we should not be defined by the color of our skin, but, as Dr. King said, by the content of our character...

One thing that really gets under my skin is when people ask, "Why won't you guys just let it go?" *Ummm... Excuse me? What do you mean?*

They'll say, "You know, this whole, like, racism thing from the past, and slavery... just let it go. C'mon. Move on! It's 2024."

I think my life and my journey is a demonstration that I've done everything I can to move on, but it's hard to move on when it follows you, when it stalks you — like I said, at opportune and inopportune times.

I've seen what happens when people have the inability to move on. ████████ is a great example, and what we did in removing those Confederate monuments flipped the script on the issue of people's inability to move on...

I was elected here in ████████ when I was ██. And, you know, there's something that I think is true for many Black leaders, and in particular Black mayors in cities across America: we have to walk a tightrope every day.

There is no harder job in America than being a Black mayor. My white counterparts don't experience the job in the way that I experience this job.

Not only do I have to be a leader for all of my residents, but I also have to be a leader within my own community, and they're counting on me to recognize the wrongs that they face in their everyday walks of life. At the same time, my White residents are sometimes requesting us to simply move forward. We are always walking a tightrope. There is less grace than you can imagine because of the conflicts that occur within our constituencies. And I see this issue within my own party as well. I'm a Democrat, and I think this issue is one that is amplified in our urban landscapes.

** end of interview **

What can be made of these responses???...???...???...

I think that both interviewees expressed earnestly held beliefs. I don't think either of them were lying to me or deploying glib artifices for the sake of staying in the good graces of their racial kin. In other words, I don't think they were holding back.

I think both of them are extremely conscious of race — conscious on a level that no mainstream White politician would ever admit to being.

It is this consciousness that makes it possible for Blacks to perceive shoulders where they do exist, but it's also this consciousness that disposes them to insist on the existence of larger, more totalizing forms of racism than the form I exposed with my hitchhiking venture.

The centers of power in the nation, somewhat ironically, also insist on the existence of larger, more totalizing forms of racism — racism that establishes itself at the institutional level.

Joe Biden *is not technically* a Black man, but there is little daylight between the way that he speaks about race and the way that the median Black politician speaks about race. And since he *is technically* the most powerful man on the planet, that kind of matters. It both reflects and contours the profile of our nation's racial landscape.

When invited to deliver the commencement speech at Howard University's 2023 graduation, Biden conveyed to the sea of Black students, family, and faculty that the larger, more totalizing forms of racism are bursting with destructive vigor. "Neo-nazis," "Klansmen," etc., etc., etc.

> *I don't have to tell you that fearless progress towards justice often meets ferocious pushback from the oldest and most sinister of forces. That's because hate never goes away.*

> *... But on the best days, enough of us have the guts and the hearts to stand up for the best in us. To choose love over hate, unity over disunion, progress over retreat. To stand up against the poison of white supremacy, as I did in my Inaugural Address — to single it out as the most dangerous terrorist threat to our homeland...*

The reason I bring up Biden remarks once again is that he really is the mouth of the American political and cultural establishment. He is the conduit through which all of the ideas of the people who matter are ejected out into the nation's spongy cultural mind.

There is no way he is personally writing any of this stuff, and I'm seriously doubtful that he believes or comprehends much of it himself, but the rhetoric is important to engage with because it perfectly encapsulates and epitomizes all of the sentiments that the most powerful people in this country wish to propagate amongst the American public. The same dynamic is ultimately at play when Vice President Harris goes on national television to decry the country's "two systems of justice." I could give countless examples. In America, the movers, shakers, leaders, and cultural tastemakers want it to be believed that institutional reform is required to address the threat of White supremacy, thereby remedying racial inequality.

Details about the desired institutional reform are, rather conspicuously, not often volunteered.

CHAPTER 21: "IT'S MORE THAN THE SHOULDERS"

"It's institutional," they will say.

What they mean, I think, is that it is elusive.

"It's more than the shoulders," they will say, upon reading this book. Again, what I think they mean is that it is elusive.

As people who are far more cynical and grating than myself have repeatedly pointed out, there is a misalignment between supply and demand in America's market for racial oppression.

Institutional racism (the anti-Black variety) is effectively dead. Moreover, many opportunities for interpersonal racism have been killed by virtue of our observant and castigatory social fabric. Most of what's left of racism in this country are the few, socially narrow opportunities for soft interpersonal racism: *shoulder racism.*

Taxonomizing the types of racism that exist in America is possible. And it's clarifying, I think, for level-headed people... Delineating the different manifestations and attempting to put them in boxes helps get us closer to an honest, pragmatic understanding of the current racial moment.

The Taxonomy of Racism

1. Institutional Racism	Interpersonal Racism	
	2. Socially Unacceptable "Hard" Interpersonal Racism	3. Socially Acceptable "Shoulder" Interpersonal Racism
Laws and organizational policies that are inherently discriminatory on the basis of race. e.g. An educational institution that maintains a policy of only admitting White students.	Perceptibly discriminatory behavior that is racial in character, that is exhibited within the confines of institutions, and that typically results in social condemnation. e.g. A hiring manager who only hires Whites despite having access to a racially diverse pool of qualified applicants.	Subtle forms of racially discriminatory behavior, typically exhibited in the personal spheres of life, that do not result in social condemnation. e.g. A driver who offers a ride to a White hitchhiker but refuses to offer a ride to a Black hitchhiker in similar circumstances.

This taxonomy serves as a functional heuristic for understanding modern racism in its manifold expressions.

Is the racism instantiated, either formally or informally, in law or policy? If yes, it is Type 1 on the chart: institutional racism. If not, it must be one of the two types of interpersonal racism.

The heuristic extends…

Is the interpersonal racism the taboo, socially impermissible sort that will result in consequences? If yes, then it's the second type of interpersonal racism on the taxonomy. If not, it's Type 3.

Generally speaking, Democrats, independents, and bluish Republicans insist that the current problem of racism is more expansive than the shoulder scenarios. They claim that Type 3 is not the only type on my taxonomy that rears its head in American life on a frequent basis. They insist — as evinced by their remarks on race, and as demonstrated by their ostensibly corrective racial policies — that racism pervades American society, not only at the interpersonal level, but also at the institutional level.

And what are these larger, institutional forms of racism? Both the congressman and the mayor made allusions that are easily graspable if you have even a cursory understanding of America's racial discourse. In America, the most prominent domains wherein institutional racism is said to perpetuate are education, criminal justice, and the workplace.

CHAPTER 22: THE SCHOOLS

There are some people who will cite the vast and undeniable disparity between the quality of primarily White schools and the quality of primarily Black schools in America as a clear example of institutional racism.

I don't believe that's sensible…

In some important respect, institutional racism in the domain of American education ended 70 years ago...

The case of *Brown v. Board of Education of Topeka* (1954) marked a truly historic, watershed moment in the saga of American civil rights and public education. It was the Supreme Court's firm rejection of racial segregation in the nation's schools.

Historically, segregation was endorsed by the 1896 *Plessy v. Ferguson* decision, which upheld the "separate but equal" doctrine under the guise of affording equal protection to Blacks. However, by the mid-20th century, a series of cases challenged this principle on the grounds that segregated facilities were inherently unequal, culminating in *Brown v. Board*. This case, a consolidation of five cases from different states led by the NAACP, presented a unified challenge to the legality of segregated schooling.

The unanimous ruling declared that state-sponsored segregation of public schools violated the Equal Protection Clause of the Fourteenth Amendment, declaring emphatically that separate educational facilities are inherently unequal. This decision engendered the gradual desegregation of schools across America and also energized the broader Civil Rights Movement, laying foundational legal groundwork that prompted subsequent reforms. By overturning *Plessy*, the Supreme Court acknowledged the profound psychological and social consequences inflicted by segregation, significantly altering the landscape of American race relations and setting a precedent for future civil rights advancements.

The *Brown v Board* ruling initiated a profound and irreversible transformation within the American educational system. Unlike any legal development theretofore, it shook the entrenched norms of racial segregation... ... ...

... However, the directive to desegregate schools across the nation also sowed the seeds of new conflicts as communities grappled with the practical implications of integration. Over the ensuing years, these tensions increasingly flared in urban areas, where diverse populations intersected with stark economic disparities and competing interests over educational control and resources. By the late 1960s, the tensions came to a head in school districts throughout the nation... particularly in dense urban centers... particularly in places like New York City...

The 1968 New York City teachers' strike became a focal point of interracial strife. It spotlit the unmistakable interplay between race, class, and education. It underscored the ongoing struggles over school governance and the allocation of educational resources, demonstrating just how deeply the ideals set forth by *Brown* had disturbed the status quo, pushing communities into new battlegrounds over how to achieve a truer form of educational equity. Throughout the '50s and '60s, Blacks were rapidly becoming majorities in places where they had previously been almost nonexistent. And accordingly, their engagement with educational institutions meant engaging with historically non-Black school districts.

The extremely factious strike of '68 centered around the Ocean Hill-Brownsville section of Brooklyn, a predominantly Black, predominantly low-income community that had been riding the cultural momentum of the broader Civil Rights Movement to advocate for greater Black involvement in school governance. In particular, the issue of whether or not the primarily White and Jewish membership of the United Federation of Teachers (UFT) were allowed to suspend students for "disruptive" behavior" was at play.[15]

The issue reached a zenith when the Ocean Hill-Brownsville local school board — a primarily Black body established by a citywide decentralization effort aimed at giving communities more control over their schools — attempted to exercise its authority by unilaterally dismissing non-Black teachers and administrators. Many of these educators were UFT members who viewed the dismissals as illegal and a violation of their union rights.

Writing in *The New York Times*, James Traub characterized the stormy repercussions of the attempted decentralization effort, which was utterly and predictably racialized from the outset:

> *It was not an absurd premise, but it was probably inevitable, at that turbulent moment, that community control played itself out in strictly racial terms. The planning council – that is, the newly established local school board – sent dismissal letters to 19 teachers and administrators, all but one of them white and Jewish. The teachers' union responded by going out on strike; a judge forced the local board to take back the teachers; and soon young men wearing Black Panther berets and bandoliers were terrorizing the teachers on the steps of J.H.S. 271 while police officers and demonstrators were fighting pitched battles in front of the school on Herkimer Street.*[16]

Indeed, J.H.S. 271 became a symbol and central battleground of this broader conflict. It was here that the local board's decision to remove staff sparked significant media attention and public outcry, leading to charges of antisemitism and racism, and intensifying the debate over who should control public education. The UFT responded with a series of citywide strikes, affecting hundreds of thousands of students and culminating in a tense standoff that lasted for several weeks.

The 1968 teachers' strike proliferated to involve the participation of over 50,000 teachers. It disrupted classes for over a month, for over a million students. At J.H.S. 271, and throughout the entire city, it exposed the complex interplay of race and educational governance. It revealed deep divisions in the city and the challenges of implementing meaningful educational reforms that addressed racial inequalities while balancing the interests of various stakeholders, including educators, unions, and local communities. It brought myriad problems to the surface of the nation's racial discourse, but it solved none of them. Primarily Black schools were dysfunctional, and Black communities were frustrated... They wanted to see institutional change... They believed that the existing institutions governing the provision of education were discriminatory against Blacks, and therefore they agitated to produce institutional change that would enhance the Black experience.

Half a century after the introduction of the community-controlled school board, half a century after the teacher walkouts, and half a century after the protestors and counter-protesters clashed on the steps of 271, the school is still totally dysfunctional. But it is not institutionally racist.

I know all of this extremely well...

I know because, not so long ago, I was a teacher at 271... I taught there at the outset of the post-Floyd era... for two seemingly interminable semesters...

It is a school where only a few kids in each class can read and write at grade level.

It is a school where the kids are constantly fighting — in the classrooms, in the hallways, and in front of the bodega across the street.

It is a school like a lot of schools in the United States.

And of the hundreds of students I taught at J.H.S. 271, not a single one was White...

... Which seems bizarre if you zoom out and think about the overall demographics of the city, and of the country at large. Hundreds of students, but not a single one who was White. A couple students would identify as Puerto Rican or Dominican, maybe, but other than that, all of them were Black.

And how were these students treated? Did we (the racially diverse faculty) treat them with the care and attention that all students deserve? I think so.

Some of the students I taught are people who I still think about to this day. I cared (and still do care) about them very deeply. Some of the students are people who I would have very much liked to see attend a better school, one that was less chaotic and more nurturing of their talents than 271 ever could be...

271 was chaotic and often quite callous. I wish it could have been better. I tried to make it better...

And while I do think I was careful and attentive as a teacher, I don't believe that care and attention are universally and always shown in Black schools. Moreover, I would not be the **least bit** surprised to read a study indicating that Black students, in general, cross paths with fewer solid-educators throughout their academic upbringing.

There are BLACKSCHOOLS ...|... There are WHITESCHOOLS.

No, segregation didn't realllllyyyyyy end with *Brown*... ...
... not in the real or statistical sense...

The American school system remains segregated today. It is not segregated by law, but it is by demographic circumstance. There are many schools like 271 where basically all of the kids are Black. These schools are almost always inferior, both in qualitative experience and in quantitative results, to the neighboring White schools.

And so the impulse to conflate this jarring inequality with the existence of institutional racism is understandably strong. It's strong because people in leadership positions are naturally disposed to be optimistic and solution oriented. After all, institutions can be reformed. Laws can be rewritten. Policies can be modernized.

But are these schools really **racist as institutions?** *Are the school boards that oversee them* **racist as institutions?** *Do they maintain laws or policies that discriminate against students on a racial basis?*

They simply can't. There are simply too many people and law firms and bureaus and organizations who work full-time to ensure that racism cannot manifest on an institutional level.

And that admission is painful, discouraging, and disorienting … obviously….

And what of post-secondary institutions?

It feels beneath me to write about the mélange of forces that make the college experience — from application to graduation — different for Blacks and Whites. Everything about it is painful, discouraging, and disorienting … obviously….

CHAPTER 23: THE JUSTICE SYSTEM

I don't even know what I'm supposed to talk about here...

Am I supposed to talk about socioeconomic factors? How high crime rates are often correlated with socioeconomic disadvantage? How poverty, lack of employment opportunities, inadequate education, and poor housing conditions are more prevalent in many Black communities due to historical economic disparities? How these conditions can lead to higher crime rates, which in turn lead to more frequent encounters with cops and higher incarceration rates? How blatant disparities in the criminal justice system are economic issues at their core, not racial ones?

I don't want to!

Am I supposed to argue that the disparities in arrest and incarceration rates arise from neutral policing policies that happen to interact with demographically skewed patterns of crime? Am I supposed to suggest that if a policy directs police to focus on areas with high drug trafficking, and those areas disproportionately house Black communities, the resulting enforcement will naturally lead to higher rates of Black arrests? Am I supposed to say that the policies are not inherently racist but rather geographically and statistically driven?

I don't want to!!

Am I supposed to mention how varying cultural norms or community dynamics like upbringing, community structures, or values about authority and law enforcement might influence interactions with police? That different historical and cultural experiences can shape how communities interact with law enforcement, independent of racial prejudice from within the system?

I don't want to!!!

Am I supposed to enter the minefield of differential involvement in crime? Am I supposed to entertain the notion that differences in crime rates among racial groups are due to factors such as age demographics? That younger populations are statistically more likely to commit crimes, and some minority communities have younger age profiles? That higher crime rates, therefore, and subsequent policing attention might reflect these demographic structures rather than interpersonal or institutional racism?

I do not want to!!!!!

Am I supposed to propose that what appears to be racial bias in policing and sentencing is instead a misinterpretation of data that fails to account for other critical variables? Do I proffer that factors like previous criminal history, the severity of the crime, and other legal variables play a role in the justice outcomes observed, and that these factors are not always adequately controlled for in analyses that highlight racial disparities?

I DO NOT WANT TO SAY ANY OF THAT !!!!!!

grazes fingers over keyboard without actually typing anything....

exhales deeply

I don't think this chapter is enough, but I also don't know if anything would be enough. The events that led us here were so blinding, painful, and psychologically disruptive.

I honestly don't know what someone is supposed to say in this section of the book.

CHAPTER 24: THE WORKPLACE

I don't know what I'm supposed to write in this section of the book either.

I think the taxonomy I designed is a useful reference. I think it provides much-needed clarity to the racial analyses of all domains of American life, including in the workplace. And so I will use it.

Are there any laws in America that specifically and explicitly discriminate against Blacks in the workplace?

I ask this in earnest, but I know a decent amount about America, and I am seriously inclined to say no.

Institutional racism simply hasn't been as strong as its opponents.

For decades, civil rights organizations such as the Southern Poverty Law Center and the National Association for the Advancement of Colored People have waged a relentless war against institutional racism.

Their efforts have spanned from challenging discriminatory laws and practices in the courts to advocating for policy changes at both the state and federal levels. Through strategic litigation, rigorous advocacy, and public education campaigns, these groups have significantly dismantled many of the systemic barriers that once perpetuated racial disparities in myriad sectors. By 2024, the landscape of institutional racism has been thoroughly transformed due to these persistent efforts. Many (if not all… and quite possibly all) of the overt structures and policies that historically disadvantaged racial minorities have been reformed or abolished, leading to a new phase of civic engagement between America's racial groups.

Today, the focus of these organizations has increasingly shifted towards addressing racial discrimination on an interpersonal level. This includes tackling subtler forms of bias and prejudice that manifest in everyday interactions, which are more elusive but continue to perpetuate a sense of division and inequality. As these groups adapt to the evolving nature of racial issues, their putative mission remains pointed: to root out racism in all its forms and foster a society that upholds the dignity and equality of every individual.

These bodies are tremendously effective. They're like an immune system. They're vigilant, responsive, and quick.

Their efforts make me think of how the government of Alberta made my birth-province the largest inhabited area in the world that is rat-free.

Much like Alberta's famously effective rat control strategy, where any sighting of a rat triggers a swift and coordinated response to eradicate the loathed intruder, civil rights organizations, in partnership with governmental allies, have established a robust system to address and extinguish instances of institutional racism. The response is predictable and nearly instant. This proactive approach mirrors the vigilance of Alberta's well-equipped "rat patrol" teams, who maintain a rat-free province through their diligence and immediate action.

In the realm of civil rights, a similar vigilance has been institutionalized. When manifestations of institutional racism are detected — be they in law, corporate practice, or systems of education — a well-oiled machine comprising civil rights organizations alongside local, state, and federal entities springs into action. This powerful, moneyed network operates under comprehensive legal frameworks and public policies that not only discourage but actively combat any identifiable form of institutional racism. Regulatory bodies, akin to Alberta's ecological watchdogs, conduct regular inspections and reviews to ensure compliance with anti-discrimination laws.

Moreover, just as Alberta educates its citizens on the importance of maintaining a rat-free environment, these organizations foster public awareness about the perils of racism, creating a culture that does not tolerate discrimination against racial minorities. Whenever something pops up, like the rare rat in Alberta, there is an immediate mobilization of resources and community action to address and resolve the issue. This systemic readiness ensures that instances of institutional racism, though they may emerge sporadically, are met with decisive action, reinforcing a societal norm where equality is maintained with high resolve. It's like an immune response.

The nature of America's media ecosystem also makes it virtually impossible for institutional racism to exist. Genuine cases of institutional racism are simply too valuable to journalists to remain in the darkness. If you manage to find one, you'll win a Pulitzer, a high-paying staff job at a legacy outlet, a prestigious think-tank fellowship, or something else of that sort. If you actually find one, your life changes overnight.

In response to historical civil rights advances, American workplaces have evolved to establish a professional paradigm where institutional racism is discouraged and structurally countered through comprehensive policies and oversight mechanisms — with obsessive alacrity, in many cases.

This transformation is evident in the widespread adoption of equal employment opportunities, affirmative action policies, and rigorous DEI initiatives within corporate and public sectors. Modern organizations are equipped with HR and DEI regimes that aggressively monitor, evaluate, and enforce these policies, ensuring that discrimination at institutional levels (in even the most remotely plausible cases) is addressed before it can grow.

Last summer, for instance, a 1.8-billion-dollar settlement was won by Black and Latino teachers in New York City whose civil rights were supposedly infringed when they were forced to take a certification exam for which failure rates were racially disparate. This sort of stuff, radical though it may seem to foreigners, is not all that unusual in the American context.

Because of historical sensitivities, there is a cultural impulse in America to conflate macro-level racial disparities with institutional injustice, and to swiftly implement legal measures in response.

Furthermore, the professional landscape now includes robust legal and regulatory frameworks that hold companies accountable for discriminatory practices that occur internally, on the interpersonal level. For instance, an individual hiring manager exhibiting racial bias — such as refusing to hire qualified Black employees — faces significant repercussions ranging from disciplinary actions by their superiors to legal consequences enforced by entities like the Equal Employment Opportunity Commission. These internal and external oversight mechanisms work in tandem to maintain a workplace environment that upholds the principles of colorblindness and equality, reflecting a dramatic shift from past decades where such discrimination went unchecked. This structured approach has created a professional culture that actively weeds out overt discrimination and subtler forms of interpersonal racism. It has rendered a working environment in which all but *shoulder racism* is gone.

In American professional life, institutional racism and explicit interpersonal racism against Blacks is effectively dead — and in the vanishing cases where it stubbornly ekes forward on life support, in the vanishing cases where its pulse hasn't completely flatlined, untold billions of dollars are going toward pulling the plug.

And the shoulder racism? How does it appear in the workforce? How do the subtle, socially acceptable forms of interpersonal racism arise in the professional sphere?

That part isn't always clear…

We all know it does play out, of course, delicately but surely, in its own understated ways...

Could we get rid of it? Do people even want to get rid of it? What would that look like? What would that entail?

CHAPTER 25: ON ZOOMERS

There is something going on with the Zoomers that feels worth discussing, if only briefly.

There is an unease... a paranoia... what many important people characterize as an angst... ... ... and a dangerous angst at that.

In contemporary American society, the implementation of affirmative action policies has catalyzed a significant cultural shift, particularly among young White men. This demographic has developed a heightened racial consciousness, one that is primarily due to the pervasiveness of affirmative action throughout their lives, intensifying notably in the past decade. These policies, which are designed to correct historical inequalities and promote diversity within institutions, have precipitated a growing backlash...

For centuries, positions of power and influence in America have predominantly been occupied by White men. This demographic hegemony went unchallenged until the latter part of the 20th century, roughly the same time as Sprigle, Griffin, and Halsell wrote their books, when affirmative action began to be widely implemented. By the time Generation Z began entering the world, these corrective measures, aimed explicitly at redressing past discrimination against minorities, were rapidly gaining momentum.

The societal shift became even more pronounced following the upheaval triggered by the death of Floyd. As I posited earlier on, 2020 marked a serious cultural inflection point. In its aftermath, there was a fervent and widespread commitment across major companies and institutions to make their demographics... for lack of a better term... less White.

And how does that happen? How do institutions become less White? If a company with 90% of its leadership positions filled by Whites vows to achieve a demographic makeup in its leadership that actually reflects the demographic makeup of the general public, what is the most likely way the company will achieve this?

Will it fire all of the existing employees and then start hiring from scratch? Do they adopt a blank slate mentality?

Of course not...

The commitment to more demographically representative institutions did not result in the dismissal of existing individuals who were White and male — from the Boomer, Gen X, and more senior Millennial cohorts — but rather, through a strategic shift in recruitment practices.

Instead of replacing current employees (older White men who have been grandfathered into secure socioeconomic perches) companies and public organizations have increasingly adopted recruitment strategies that effectively place young White men at a disadvantage. The objective is clear: to reshape the workforce demographic over time, aligning it more closely with the nation's racial diversity without disrupting the existing workforce hierarchy.

In one Bloomberg analysis that looked at data from companies in the S&P 100, it was revealed that 94% of new jobs created between 2020 and 2021 went to non-Whites, including a disproportionate number of executive and managerial positions.[17]

Whites have been an extremely dominant group in America for centuries — both economically and in sheer demographic terms. That dominance is eroding, quickly, and so efforts to "catch up for lost time" entail extreme forms of social engineering...

Again, I'm trying not to moralize here. Whether or not I think these trends are morally just in the grand historical scheme isn't all that important. I offer these remarks as a phlegmatic description of what is going on.

This ostensibly justice-oriented societal movement to correct demographics has led to a peculiar socioeconomic burden for Whites of the younger Millennial and Gen Z cohorts. They find themselves as the primary bearers of the historical weight of discrimination — discrimination that they did not personally perpetuate but that they are indirectly held accountable for due to their skin color. It's a historical irony where the sins of forefathers are being atoned for in the lives of their descendants, young men who face a corporate and societal structure significantly different from what was navigated by previous generations.

The response among these younger White men ranges from a meek reassessment of their roles within a rapidly changing social order, to outraged feelings of disenfranchisement and indignation. For this latter group, the sense of being unfairly disadvantaged for historical wrongs creates a crescendo of resentment and confusion, compounded by the fear of diminished prospects for their professional and academic aspirations. Rather predictably, it has engendered the cultural conditions necessary for the emergence of zealous dissident youth movements.

If you know anything about the internal dynamics of the Republican Party, you know that the schism dividing primarily Boomer and Gen X Neocons from primarily Millenial and Zoomer G******s is shaping up to be the GOP's defining conflict.

And if you know anything about the community guidelines of the social media companies that are necessary to have at one's disposal when distributing a book, you know why I am forced to use asterisks, and you know why it would be stupid for me to write about this schism in greater detail.

CHAPTER 26: INTRO TO CONCLUSION

A profound transformation has occurred within American institutions to accelerate racial diversity, achieving levels of integration that would have been unimaginable in previous decades. My grandfather couldn't have predicted this world, and neither could his son.

From corporate boardrooms and academic departments to political offices and newsrooms, non-White minorities, particularly Blacks, have realized staggering civic progress. American institutions now actively engage in policies geared toward enhancing diversity with the goal of reflecting the country's composite demographic mosaic.

Despite these institutional advancements, a pervasive undercurrent of interpersonal, soft racism remains entrenched in the daily experiences of many individuals. This form of soft, *shoulder racism* is subtler, manifesting not through overt policies or laws but through social interactions and personal biases. A Black man hitchhiking may face significantly longer wait times and more suspicions solely based on racial stereotypes, a reflection of enduring prejudices that no law has fully eradicated — nor does it seem likely that any law ever will.

To some extent, the subjection to shoulder racism is an intrinsic feature of being a minority in any society. Historical and comparative analyses show us that minority groups, whether defined by race, ethnicity, or religion, will always experience some form of marginalization or discrimination. They will be treated differently, on average, than members of the majority group. This is not unique to the United States; it is a global phenomenon observed in a wide range of cultural and national contexts. Racial minorities in European countries like France or Germany, for example, have different experiences than those of ethnic Frenchmen or Germans. Caste-based minorities in India, likewise, face undeniable prejudices that stem from deep-seated stereotypes and historical biases.

There is not now, nor has there ever been, an exception to this abiding natural law.

???

What can be gleaned from Seven Shoulders?

After reading the work of my predecessors…   after applying the foundation… after wearing the wig and the contact lenses… after the hours on the side of the road…. after the writing…. after creating my taxonomy of racism for the world to see………

After all of it, I do believe that two conclusions from my book stand out above the rest:

1. **In America, hitchhiking is harder for Black men than it is for White men.**

2. **In America, nobody is forced to hitchhike.**

I realize, of course, that these conclusions may sound glib. I realize that they may sound flippant. I realize that they may come across as curt and insufficiently reflective.

But they are actually very serious and profound conclusions…

Yes, *shoulder racism* exists. Just as it existed on the side of the roadways where I attempted to solicit rides, so too does it exist in other areas of American life. It exists in dating behavior. It exists in the formation of friend groups. It permeates the nation's consumption of food, clothing, and art. Deeply ingrained racial biases exist in all Americans, and a fundamental feature of the American experience is the personal liberty that allows those biases to manifest.

But the veracity of the second conclusion minimizes the racially disparate damnation of the first. Blacks are protected from leading their lives exclusively on the shoulders. They are protected by the vast availability of options and alternatives… As is the case for all minorities, they are rarely forced to rely on the goodwill or personal conjecture of Whites in order to lead flourishing lives... ... ... because they are protected...

They are protected by popular social sentiment and enforceable laws. They are protected because they live in America, a country that has been shaped by decades of structural reform and attitudinal renaissance, both of which have shrunk the range of socially acceptable racism to an extent that is globally unprecedented — and moreover, to an extent that may be terminal if America is to retain the reputation of personal liberty that distinguishes it as the country that is different from all the other countries...

REFERENCES

1. Newman, R.K., (1994) *Hugo Black: A Biography*. Pantheon Books, p. 247-249.

2. *Eyewitness 1940: Pittsburgh reporter sees London Blitz up close*. Gazette. (2015, October 19). https://www.post-gazette.com/news/nation/2015/10/25/Eyewitness-1940-Pittsburgh-reporter-sees-London-Blitz-up-close/stories/201510250043

3. Sprigle, R., (1949). *In the Land of Jim Crow*. Simon and Schuster.

4. Griffin, J. H., Terkel, S., Bonazzi, R., & Rutledge, D. (2006). *Black Like Me: The definitive griffin estate edition*. Wings Press.

5. Griffin-Bonazzi, E. (n.d.). *Griffin, John Howard*. Texas State Historical Association. https://www.tshaonline.org/handbook/entries/griffin-john-howard

6. Halsell, G., (1969). *Soul Sister*. The World Publishing Company.

7. Woo, E. (2000, August 21). *Grace Halsell; author, impersonated black, wrote "Soul sister."* Los Angeles Times. https://www.latimes.com/archives/la-xpm-2000-aug-21-me-7932-story.html

8. Hoffman, B., Mather, V., & Fortin, J. (2017, September 24). *After trump blasts N.F.L., players kneel and lock arms in Solidarity. The New York Times*. https://www.nytimes.com/2017/09/24/sports/nfl-trump-anthem-protests.html

9. Gould, E., & Wilson, V. (2020, June 1). *Black workers face two of the most lethal preexisting conditions for coronavirus-racism and economic inequality*. Economic Policy Institute. https://www.epi.org/publication/black-workers-

covid#:~:text=Black%20workers%20saw%20slightly%20grea
ter,jobs%20between%20February%20and%20April

10. *Bank of America announces $1 billion/4-year commitment to support Economic Opportunity Initiatives*. Bank of America. (2020, June 2). https://newsroom.bankofamerica.com/content/newsroom/pre ss-releases/2020/06/bank-of-america-announces--1-billion-4-year-commitment-to-suppor.html

11. *JPMorgan Chase commits $30 billion to advance racial equity*. JPMorgan Chase Commits $30 Billion to Advance Racial Equity. (2020, October 8). https://www.jpmorganchase.com/ir/news/2020/jpmc-commits-30-billion-to-advance-racial-equity

12. Konell, J. (2022). Bike Life, Cultural Conflict, and The City. *University of Pennsylvania Journal of Law and Social Change*, 25(3), 201–207. https://scholarship.law.upenn.edu/cgi/viewcontent.cgi?article =1272&context=jlasc

13. Arsenault, R., (2006) *Freedom Riders: 1961 and the Struggle for Racial Justice*. Oxford University Press, p. 138.

14. *Encyclopedia of Detroit*. Detroit Historical Society . (n.d.). https://detroithistorical.org/learn/encyclopedia-of-detroit/grand-bargain

15. Ravitch, D. (2000). *The Great School Wars: A History of the New York City Public Schools*. Johns Hopkins University Press.

16. Traub, J. (2002, October 6). *A lesson in unintended consequences*. The New York Times. https://www.nytimes.com/2002/10/06/magazine/a-lesson-in-unintended-consequences.html

17. Bloomberg Businessweek. (2023, September 25). *Corporate America Promised to Hire a Lot More People of Color. It Actually Did*. Bloomberg.com. https://www.bloomberg.com/graphics/2023-black-lives-matter-equal-opportunity-corporate-diversity/

Made in the USA
Columbia, SC
03 August 2024